MIDLANDS

Edited by Annabel Cook

CW00497182

First published in Great Britain in 2003 by
YOUNG WRITERS
Remus House,
Coltsfoot Drive,
Peterborough, PE2 9JX
Telephone (01733) 890066

All Rights Reserved

Copyright Contributors 2003

SB ISBN 1 84460 299 0

FOREWORD

Young Writers was established in 1991 as a foundation for promoting the reading and writing of poetry amongst children and young adults. Today it continues this quest and proceeds to nurture and guide the writing talents of today's youth.

From this year's competition Young Writers is proud to present a showcase of the best poetic talent from across the UK. Each hand-picked poem has been carefully chosen from over 66,000 'Hullabaloo!' entries to be published in this, our eleventh primary school series.

This year in particular we have been wholeheartedly impressed with the quality of entries received. The thought, effort, imagination and hard work put into each poem impressed us all and once again the task of editing was a difficult but enjoyable experience.

We hope you are as pleased as we are with the final selection and that you and your family will continue to be entertained with *Hullabaloo! Midlands* for many years to come.

CONTENTS

Georgia Cash (9)	52
Nicola Pitt (10)	53
Matthew Walker (10)	54
Natasha Bodenham (10)	55
Hannah Shaw (9)	56
Loveen Dyall (9)	57
Abigail Lamond (9)	57
Grace Carrington (10)	58
Jessica Lear (11)	58
Chloe Bates (10)	59
Danielle Duggan (10)	60
Joanne Shepherd (10)	61

Colley Lane Primary School, Halesowen

Jade Hitchcock (8)	61
Bryony Crumpton (8)	62
Daniel Crowe (9)	62
James Taylor (8)	63
Daniel Parsons (8)	63
Amy Blount (9)	64
Gameel Maged (8)	64
Hannah Smallpage-Hurst (8)	64
Elizabeth Dear (9)	65
Charlie Carrington (9)	65
Derrie Pearson (9)	65
Tammie Foster (8)	66
Holly Harvey (9)	66
Stacie Hingley (9)	66
Sam Resuggan (9)	67
Bethany Turner (8)	67

Dingle Community Primary School, Kingswinford

Jessica Bird (10)	67
Bradley Ghent (10)	68
Sarah-Jayne Garbett (10)	68
Claire Farmer (10)	69
Hannah Penn (10)	69
Amy Smith (10)	70

Rachael Platt (10)	70
Jemima Winwood (10)	70
Robert Mutch (10)	71
Zak Westwood (10)	71
Joshua Rock (10)	72
Alison Starkey (9)	72
Daniel Rock (10)	73
Abby Jones (10)	73
Jordan Danks (9)	74
Rebekah Garbett (10)	74
Sarah Potter (9)	75
Andrew Rogerson (9)	75
Thomas Nicholson (9)	76
Joseph Haden (9)	76
Sophia Dimopaulou (9)	77
Elliot Westwood (9)	77
Daniel Fellows (9)	78
Daniel Lamb (9)	78
Kieran Bates (8)	78
Benjamin Jones (9)	79
Emily Fisher (9)	79
Rachel Wood (9)	80
Sarina Lad (8)	80
Kimberley Fennell (8)	80
Christopher Round (9)	81
James Baxter (8)	81
Jodi Cooper (8)	81
Chloe Gillard (9)	82
Martin Siviter (9)	82
Amy Davies (8)	83
Hayley Siviter (9)	83
Stefanie Ward (8)	83
Rhianna Davies (10)	84
Cole Hickman (8)	84
Chloe Rutherford (8)	85
Chloe Ghent (7)	85
Amy Potter (7)	85
Jenna Smith (10)	86

Alice Maycock (7)	86
Hannah Williams (7)	86
Tom Southall (10)	87

English Martyrs RC Primary School, Oakham

Ciara Dullaghan (9)	87
Amy Longhurst (9)	88
Callum Quigley (9)	88
Rosie Besant (9)	89
Charlie Robertson (10)	89
Thomas Caldicott (11)	90
Laura Miller (10)	90
Joseph Nerini (10)	91
Eleanor Mitchell (10)	91
Oliver Phipps (11)	92
Joe Longhurst (9)	92
Ryan Quinn (11)	93
Tom Stafford (11)	93
Jonathan Forster (10)	94

George Betts Primary School, Smethwick

Zoe Wood (10)	94
Rheanne Bailey (11)	95
Sam Lundy (10)	96
Kirsty Louise Macdonald (10)	97
Sandeep Ghuman (10)	98
Jaspreet Kaur (10)	99
Louise Harris (11)	100
Anisha Kumari (10)	101
Jasdeep Matharu (11)	102
Raveena Gill (11)	103

Glenmere CP School, Wigston

Jake Haston (8)	103
Freya Vincent (8)	104
Hafsah Ali (8)	105
Stefan Bullous (8)	105
Josh Kirk (8)	106

Rose Ashton (8)	106
Jordan Wills (8)	106
Jamie Wright (8)	107
Arthur Redfern (9)	107
Jessica Cooper (8)	108
William Haston (8)	108
Nisha Gorania (8)	109
Katie Deacon (9)	109
Freddie Dobrijevic (9)	110
Frankie Sharman (9)	110
Kathryn Reynolds (9)	110
Amy Brown (8)	111
Oliver Stone (8)	111
Aimee Harris (9)	111
Jodie Langley (9)	112

Hurst Green Primary School, Halesowen

Hannah Stevens (9)	112
Katie Danks (8)	113
Antonia Veal (9)	113
Oliver Rogers (8)	114
Tyler Shutts (8)	114
David Alsop (8)	115
Laura Hayfield (9)	115
Benjamin Timmington-Taylor (9)	116
Ben Kirton (9)	116
Joshua Collett (9)	117
Arran Dhillon (8)	117
Joseph Rose (9)	118
Tom Blears (8)	118
Bradley Clarke (8)	119
James Wythes (8)	119
Isaac Kelly (8)	120
Christian Goodgame (8)	120
James Hanson (8)	120
Kyra Rai (9)	121
Andrew Irving (9)	121
Daniel Marsh (8)	122

Rebekah Swain (9)   122
Leah Eckesley (8)   122
Alex Byatt (8)   123
Amy Davies (8)   123
Jagpreet Ghuman (9)   124
Jamie Gill (9)   124
Jordan Gibbs (8)   125
Ben Churchill (8)   125
Alex Cox (9)   126
Megan Evans (9)   126
Sara Lee (9)   127
Adam Scott (8)   127
Rebecca Hanley (8)   128
Ryan Wainwright (9)   128
Holly McKnight (9)   129
Joseph Upton (8)   129
Jamie O'Toole (9)   130
Conor Devaney (8)   130
Grant Meredith (9)   131
Lewis Carey (9)   131
James Burton (8)   132
Becky Hale (10)   132
Liam Gray (9)   133
Chloe Edwards (8)   133
Stephen Scott (10)   134
Laura Mayes (10)   134
Cory Laidlaw (10)   134
Sophie Byatt (10)   135
Jonathan Guy (10)   135
Tom Kavanagh (10)   135
Georgina Rowe (10)   136
Mandeep Johal (10)   136
Kirsty Slater (9)   136
Amanda Smith (9)   137
Katie Manison (10)   137
Sunjay Virdee (10)   137
Megan Loone (9)   138
Meera Nayyar (9)   138

Thomas Stanley (9)	159
Nicolle Birkin (9)	159
Tom King (9)	160
Jenna Crompton (8)	160
Paige Walsh (8)	161
Thomas Shakespeare (9)	161
Michael Bradshaw (9)	162
Ryan Firman (8)	162
Justin Stinson (8)	163
Ben Fox (8)	163
James Bayley (9)	164
James Dwyer (9)	164
Rhea Smith (9)	165
Rosie Adams (9)	165
Michael Topping (9)	166
Bethany Thompson (8)	166
Rose Goldman (9)	167

Mount Pleasant Primary School, Brierley Hill

Tiffany Johnstone (8)	167
Priyesh Patel (8)	168
Josh Lambe (9)	168
Georgia Williams (8)	169
Bethany-Rose Madkins (9)	170
Lily Staves (8)	171
Rikesh Patel (9)	171
Simone Round (9)	172
Shardae McDonald (9)	172
Kate Adams (9)	173
Ben Carrington (9)	174
Ryan North (9)	174
Katie North (9)	175
Liam Bradley (8)	176
Louise Pinnell (9)	176
Daniel Appleton (8)	177
Laura Taylor (8)	177
Amie Adams (8)	178
Sasha Guest (10)	178

Matthew Reese (8)	179
Alison Clarke (10)	179
Jasmine Worsfold (9)	180
Jordan Madkins (10)	180
Michael Pearson (9)	181
Charlotte Prosser (11)	181
Kirsty Tolley (11)	182
Stephanie Wheeldon (10)	182
Jodie Cox (10)	183
Rebecca Hemmings (11)	183
Elisha Caldwell (11)	184
Robert Bloomer (10)	184
Laura Banks (11)	185
Kirstie Taylor (10)	186
Stacey Crook (11)	187
Kristopher Fellows (10)	187
Samuel Freestone (8)	188
Faye Bradley (11)	188
Daniel Such (10)	189
Aaron Chawro (11)	190
Thomas Taylor (7)	191
Louisa Hampson (7)	192
Bethany Smith (8)	193
Daniel Layland (7)	194
Connor Brinsdon (7)	195
Danielle Baker (8)	196
Kate Paynter (7)	197
Adam Lambe (7)	198
Gemma Raybould (8)	199
Olivia Fullwood (8)	200
Krtistina Evans (9)	201
Thomas Wilkins (10)	202
Sarah Redding (9)	203
Elyse Evers (10)	204
Rebecca Godwin (10)	205
Laura Harkin (10)	206
Dominic Priest (8)	206
Abbie Morgan (8)	207

Aaran Tranter (8)   208
Lewis Girling (8)   209
Rebecca Shaw (7)   210
Laura Whitehead (7)   211
Katie-Jo Clarke (8)   212
Andrew Raybould (7)   213
Lorna Watts (8)   213
Josie Cartwright (8)   214
Shantelle McDonald (7)   214
Daniel Lander (7)   215
Amelia Evers (8)   216
Georgina Dawes (8)   216
Charlie Heaton (7)   217
Emma Paynter (10)   218
Lisa Henderson (10)   219
Ben Pedley (10)   220
Matthew Mifsud (9)   221
Zoe Nock (10)   222
Luke Beresford (10)   223

St Anne's RC Primary School, Sutton Coldfield
Danielle Howard (8)   223
Tom Wright (8)   224
Natalie Whitehouse (9)   224
Lucia Thornton (8)   224
Grace Saunderson (8)   225
Lauren Stevenson (9)   225
Adam Rattigan (9)   225
Amelia Pedley (8)   226
Emily Minchin (8)   226
Chloe Matthews (9)   226
Adam Goldthorp (8)   227
Daniel O'Doherty (9)   227
Rhys Jones (8)   228
Sam Griffith-Allen (9)   228
Cameron Gemmell (8)   228
Blane Cremin-Cullen (9)   229
James Graydon (8)   229

Hannah Dunne (9)	230
Tadeusz Forys (8)	230
Megan Humphrey (8)	230
Sarina Samra (8)	231
Ryan Brough (9)	231
Seamus Delaney (8)	231
Toby Duckworth (8)	232
George Bentley (8)	232
James Groves (8)	233
Marek Barnes (9)	233
Jamie Brannigan (8)	234
Jonathan Hobbs (8)	234
Bethany Hague (8)	235
Emma O'Hanlon (8)	236
Bethany Canavan (8)	236

St Martin's CE Primary School, Bilston

Jamie Guest (10)	237
Nicole Pearson (10)	237
Mitchell Keown (9)	237
Laura Price (10)	238
Laura Pearce (11)	238
Lauren Timmins (10)	239
Sophie Richards (10)	239
Sian Callaghan (11)	240
Aaron Asprey (8)	240
Jamie Arrowsmith (10)	240
Amy Shepherd (11)	241
Cleveland McGrory (8)	242
Holly Albutt (8)	242
Christopher Bryan & Louie Pullen (9)	243

St Peter's Primary School, Melton Mowbray

Benjamin Conboy (8)	243
James Campbell (8)	244
Nicholas Beech (9)	244
Connell Watkins (10)	245

The Poems

PLEASE MISS DAVIES

(Based on 'Please Mrs Butler' by Allan Ahlberg)

'Please Miss Davies,
This girl Lucy Loo
She keeps on talking
What shall I do?'

'Go up in space my dear
Go and move away
Go and lie down my dear
But don't ask me.'

'Please Miss Davies,
This girl Lucy Loo
She keeps on kicking me
What shall I do?'

'Go down town my dear
Go on the loo,
Go in the sink my dear
But don't ask me.'

'Please Miss Davies,
This girl Lucy Loo
She keeps pinching my stickers
What shall I do?'

'Go and hide away my dear,
Go to the shops,
Go anywhere you want my dear
But don't ask me.'

Jordan Tompkins *(8)*
Blackwood School, Sutton Coldfield

COUNTING POEM

Ten little children
All drinking wine,
One got screaming drunk,
And then there were nine.

Nine little children,
All lifting weights,
One dropped one on his toes,
And then there were eight.

Eight little children
Meeting Trevor,
One went off with him,
And then there were seven.

Seven little children
Eating pic 'n' mix,
One got sick,
And then there were six.

Six little children
All getting ready to dive,
One fell flat on his back,
And then there were five.

Five little children
Breaking the law,
One went to prison,
And then there were four.

Four little children,
All breaking their knees,
One went to hospital,
And then there were three.
Three little children
Had some gum to chew,
One swallowed it,
And then there were two.

Two little children,
Both weighing a ton,
One fell down
And then there was one.

One little child
By a kidnapper got caught,
He ran away
And then there were nought.

Katie Longmore (7)
Blackwood School, Sutton Coldfield

MY BABY BROTHER

I have a baby brother
And Ryan is his name
And since he first arrived
Life has never been the same.
He likes to shout and run away
Whenever there's a chance,
And when the music starts to play,
He really likes to dance.

Whenever I come home from school
He laughs and waves at me
And then he comes to greet me
And sits upon my knee.

We really are so lucky
For love is there to see
With our very loving parents
The dog, Ryan and
          Me.

Nicole Thompson (9)
Blackwood School, Sutton Coldfield

UNTITLED

Ten little children,
All drinking wine,
One got drunk,
And then there were nine.

Nine little children,
All lifting weights,
One dropped one on his toes,
And then there were eight.

Eight little children
Floating up to Heaven,
Then came an aeroplane,
And then there were seven.

Seven little children,
Picking up sticks,
One fell over,
And then there were six.

Six little children,
Found a beehive,
One got stung,
And then there were five.

Five little children,
Sat on the floor,
One stood up,
And then there were four.

Four little children,
Climbing up a tree,
One fell down,
And then there were three.
Three little children,
Went to the zoo,
One got lost,
And then there were two.

Two little children,
Having fun,
One started crying,
And then there was one

One little child,
Living in the sun,
One fell asleep,
And then there were none.

Jessica O'Leary (8)
Blackwood School, Sutton Coldfield

UNDER THE SEAS

Seals, seals
They act like weasels,
Seals, seals,
They should be careful not to catch the measles.
They swim under the sea,
Unlike me, but they can't count to three!
Seals, seals,
They hate things with wheels.
Here come the larks
Oh no! here come the sharks!
The seaweed is swishing
The men are fishing
Now the day is over
But I still haven't found a four-leafed clover.
The sun is down
But it had no golden crown.
So goodnight to the sea and the sky
And everything as small as a fly.

Natalie Rhodes (8)
Blackwood School, Sutton Coldfield

OUR FUTURE

What will the world
be like
when I grow up?

Will there be
pure air to breathe?
Will the sea be fresh?

Will houses
cover all the fields?
Will they still be green?

Will cows
still produce milk?
Will there be any fruit to eat?

Will whales survive
and black rhinos live?
Will there be any animals alive?

Will adults have
left us anything
living and healthy?

Will trees
be cut down
and rainforests destroyed?

Will there
be people on the streets
or will they be polluted?

When we're grown up
and we're in charge,
what will the Earth be like?

When the goodness
is all used up
will there be life on Earth?

Thomas Duggan (9)
Blackwood School, Sutton Coldfield

MY FAMILY

My family are different in special ways
Here are people in my family I'm telling you today.

Me, I'm beautiful and kind
My mom doesn't really mind
My brother called George is a pest
My daddy just flows with the rest.
My other brother called Carl always acts cool.
Michelle and Richard kissing in the pool.
Nanny is always reading her books
Grandad trying to keep his looks.
Cousin James playing with his toy,
Cousin Gemma is just pure joy.
Auntie Zeta's always relaxed,
My uncle Joey has a dog called Max.
My other auntie called Jean, being lazy,
Makes my uncle Les go crazy.

That's my family each and everyone
And they are the crowd that makes me proud.

Katie Crowther (9)
Blackwood School, Sutton Coldfield

OUR FUTURE

What will our world be like
in my grown-up life?

Will birds still fly
in the blue, blue sky?

Will whales sing
or will we need to say goodbye?

Will animals still be alive
like elephants or rhinoceros?

Will mankind survive
in our changing world?

Will fields still exist
or will they be covered in tarmac?

Will the air be full of mist
or the fumes of the cars?

Will the sea be full of litter
like cans and bags?

How will *you* make
the world fitter?

Jack Shaw (8)
Blackwood School, Sutton Coldfield

OUR FUTURE

What will be
left here for me
when I grow up?

Is there going to be
any pure air to breathe?
Is there clean calm sea?

Are the green fields
going to be tarmac?
Will the fields be all grey?

Will the food be healthy
like meat and veg?
Are we going to eat them all?

Will the sun turn dark?
Will the car fumes spoil
all the world around us?

Will the whales be poisoned
and elephants too?
Will other animals survive?

Have you left anything
healthy for me and you?

Have they left us any
fresh water to drink?

If you have used the goodness up
and have you destroyed the world?

Emma Lowe (8)
Blackwood School, Sutton Coldfield

PLAYING IN THE SUN

Playing in the sun,
Having lots of fun.
Kicking a ball,
Against the wall.

Looking in the shed,
I see spiders dead.
Trying to find my bike,
Which I really like.

Swinging on the swing,
Having a lovely sing.
I will never stop,
Until I reach the top.

Jessica Cottrell (8)
Blackwood School, Sutton Coldfield

AUTUMN IS COMING

Autumn is the brightest season,
Now let me tell you the reason.
Falling leaves are coming fast,
Autumn is here at last!

Kicking through the autumn leaves,
As you feel the autumn breeze.
Red, yellow, orange and brown,
Autumn is falling all around.

Dark, dreary, damp and cold
All leaves die as they grow old.
In autumn time leaves change colour
Starting bright, turning duller.

Elizabeth Mallett (8)
Blackwood School, Sutton Coldfield

SWEETS AND MIDNIGHT FEASTS

I'm writing this poem for Hullabaloo,
So let me show you what I can do.
When I can't get to sleep,
And feel I'm part of a heap.
I'm in need of a good kind of sweet
To start to bring up the heat.

Maybe I might have a fizzy key,
To try and fizz up me,
Then I'll have a rolo,
Maybe a white polo.

So every week I'll have feasts,
To keep away all the beasts,
Then I won't be in a heap
And hopefully I'll fall fast asleep.

Verity Peake (9)
Blackwood School, Sutton Coldfield

AUTUMN

Autumn is the brightest season
Now I will tell you the reason
Falling leaves are brilliant colours
Orange, red, gold and brown.
I'm looking forward to autumn
I'm looking forward to bright colours
But when it's winter they look much duller.
Autumn leaves prepare to die
The branches on the trees start to sigh.
Because they will soon be bare
There will be no leaves left on there.

Thomas Jones (9)
Blackwood School, Sutton Coldfield

MY FUTURE

What will the future be like
When I am older?

Will animals be extinct?
Will trees still be here for us?

Will children go outside
Or will it hurt their eyes?

Will crops still grow
Or will they be too low?

So what will the future be like
When I grow up?

Will water still be clean
Or will it be green?

Will food still be fit to eat
Or will it be sloppy and mean?

Will the earth be fresh and clean
Or will it be dull and grey?

So I ask what will the future be like?

Ella Thornton (9)
Blackwood School, Sutton Coldfield

My Family

I am clever
Daddy doesn't like wet weather
Jessie has the looks
Mommy likes her books
Grandma's in the car
While Grandpa's up the bar
Nanny serves the food
While Grandad's in a mood
Ryan kicks the ball
Nick's very small
Barry can cook
Jayne has a look
Claire can get cold
Cameron's seven months old
Craig makes gardens look bold
Emma's just gone on a honeymoon to
Mexico
I asked Ashley if I could go but he said,
'No!'

Megan Phillips (8)
Blackwood School, Sutton Coldfield

The Best Rabbit Ever

I have a little rabbit and Thumper is his name,
He is black and white and very sweet
and likes to play a game.
I sit him on my knee at night
And my love for him I send.
For he is great, my special mate,
But most of all, my friend.

Christopher Fisher (9)
Blackwood School, Sutton Coldfield

THE COUNTRYSIDE CODE

Drop your litter everywhere
All the animals try to scare
Open the gates and leave them flapping
Remember to drop all your wrapping
Always smoke and start some fires
It's okay to climb over wires
Stay off the paths, throw some rocks
Give the birds a nasty shock.

If you do all this just let me say
You're behaving in a horrible way
If you do the opposite to this rhyme
You'll have a wonderful and happy time
The countryside is a fantastic place
Let's keep it that way for the human race.

Thomas Davies (9)
Blackwood School, Sutton Coldfield

FAIRGROUND FUN

H is for happiness when we go to the fair
U is for umbrella so I don't wet my hair
L is for log flume where I get very wet
L is for lollipop which if I'm lucky I'll get
A is for action when I go on a ride
B is for bravery as I do not run and hide
A is for awesome as the rides are so fast
L is for laughter as we want it to last
O is for outstanding views from the Ferris wheel up high
O is for *oh no!*
    It's time to say goodbye.

Liam Hughes (9)
Blackwood School, Sutton Coldfield

ROCK ON DJ

It's a party tonight,
I think it's all right
For a DJ 'rocking' all day.

I'm at the party it's the best,
In fact it's better than all the rest,
The DJ is here so give a big cheer.

The DJ put on rock 'n' roll
Someone did a gambol!
My friends are here all cool.

There's a song called 'So Long',
But a person sang it all wrong.
That was the best.

Liam Atkins (8)
Blackwood School, Sutton Coldfield

HULLABALOO POEM

H   is for Hannah who plays all the day
U   is for Uncle who acts in a play
L   is for Lauren who sits on the floor
L   is for Laura who stands by the door
A   is for Adam who plays with the cat
B   is for Becky who sits on the mat
A   is for Anna who swims really well
L   is for Lucy who rings the church bell
O   is for Olivia who just doesn't care
O   is for Oliver who doesn't share.

Isabella Powell (9)
Blackwood School, Sutton Coldfield

I LOVE THE SNOW

I love the snow
how it falls from the sky
it's white and soft
but tomorrow I'll have to say goodbye.

I love the snow
how it covers the grass,
I like having a snowball fight
with my friends Mark and Shazz.

I love the snow
how soft and light it is
I like to build snowmen
for my brother named Chris.

I love the snow
but my second cousin hates it,
she hates snowballs too
because she always gets hit.

I love the snow
I have sneaked outside
when my mom comes out
I will go and hide.

I love the snow
I have invited my friends around
A friend called Matt
has brought his greyhound.

Lee Finn (8)
Blackwood School, Sutton Coldfield

PLANE PARTS

L is for Lancaster
   which bombed in World War II.
A is for America
   was fought in the war with us.
N is for navigation
   which helps the pilot find the way around
C is for crew which are with the guns
A is for aircraft
   which carries so many bombs
S is for support
   which helps the Lancaster
T is for turrets
   which shoots down enemy aircrafts
E is for engines
   which power the plane
R is for rudders
   which steer the plane.

Shaun Wark (8)
Blackwood School, Sutton Coldfield

HULLABALOO

H is for Holly who eats lots and lots
U is for Uncle who cleans lots of pots
L is for Luke who cries all the time
L is for Liam who can make a crime
A is for Andy who gets in trouble
B is for Ben who burst his bubble
A is for Adam who climbs trees
L is for Lucy who plays with leaves
O is for Oliver who reads at a lake
O is for Oscar who bakes lots of cakes.

Chris Vickers (8)
Blackwood School, Sutton Coldfield

TIGGER THE FOOTBALLER CAT!

Tigger is a footballer cat, he is called the king of cool,
when he goes out on to the pitch, he makes Beckham look like a fool.

He plays with all the best teams,
Man U, and when he plays he is rough and mean.

Tigger, Tigger, there is no one like this cool cat,
for you will see him, jumping or skipping not sleeping on a mat.

When photographs are needed to show the latest fashion,
the press will contact Tigger for looking cool and handsome is
his passion.

His fur is black and sooty and he is big and slim,
to make sure he keeps in shape he is always down the gym.

Tigger, Tigger, there is no one like this cool cat,
for you will see him, jumping or skipping not sleeping on a mat.

Rachael Hemus (11)
Blackwood School, Sutton Coldfield

HULLABALOO

H   is for Holly whose hair is very long
U   is for Uncle who sings a very nice song
L   is for Lauren who is very, very bright
L   is for Liam who stays up all night
A   is for Ann who is very cute
B   is for Ben who has a newt
A   is for Adam whose got black hair
L   is for Linda who is kind and fair
O   is for Oliver who is very brave
O   is for Olivia who loves waves.

Jessica McMullan (8)
Blackwood School, Sutton Coldfield

THE SUN

In the early bright morn,
Sun wakes up at the crack of dawn.
For after the moon has gone to bed,
Sun is here instead.
Hot as lava, yellow as yolk,
Sun shines down on happy folk.
At midday still shining strong,
Sun will shine all day long.
At places, resorts, Blackpool, Cornwall,
Sun is still standing tall.
In the evening sun is going down,
People walking out of town
Hiding behind trees as it goes,
Where is it going? Who knows?
As you draw the curtains and put on your night gown,
The moon has come up and the sun has gone down.

Zoë Spencer (10)
Blackwood School, Sutton Coldfield

HULLABALOO

H is for Harry who scores all the time
U is for Uncle who always does a mime
L is for Liam who jumped in the leaves
L is for Laura who faces her fears
A is for Anthony who likes being clever
B is for Bethany who doesn't like weather
A is for Adam who misses his Eve
L is for Luke who is naive
O is for Olie who licks his lolly
O is for Olivia who loves her dolly.

Joseph Parke (8)
Blackwood School, Sutton Coldfield

WHAT WOULD OUR FUTURE BE LIKE?

What would our future be like
when I grow up?

Would there still be trees to
get air from?

Would the sea still be
clean to play in?

Would fruit still be
ripe enough to eat?

Would we all
have a drought?

Would we be safe
if we got attacked?

Would we die
of hunger?

Would everybody
be really sad and miserable?

Would people go everywhere
and stink?

What would the world be
like when we grow up?

Jade Gutteridge (8)
Blackwood School, Sutton Coldfield

MY MESSY ROOM

Toothbrush in my side drawer,
dress and knickers on the floor
bag in the pathway of my bedroom door.

Curtains half open
my night light still on
tidy up for pocket money
Hmm what a con.

I've pulled the covers up on my bed
to cover all the toys
and turned my keyboard really low
so as not to make a noise.

At a glance Mom won't notice
the mess she cannot see
I'll find time later
perhaps tomorrow after tea.

Penelope Hodges (10)
Blackwood School, Sutton Coldfield

HULLABALOO

H   is for Hanna who plays with her hair
U   is for Una who eats lots of pears
L   is for Liam who plays a guitar
L   is for Lee who's been very far
A   is for Alice who hiccups all day
B   is for Betty who was born in May
A   is for Addam who chases the girls
L   is for Lucke who likes pearls
O   is for Olive who plays with me
O   is for Olga who has a cup of *tea*.

Scarlet Bowles (8)
Blackwood School, Sutton Coldfield

My Grandad

Sinks down into his favourite chair
Like the Titanic sinking into the water.
Always starting sentences with 'During the war . . .'
Or 'In my day . . .'
His eyes are glass glinting in the sunlight
His face a maze of wrinkles, his nose the centre
His deep booming voice rings out like a school bell.
His laugh is as comforting as a cuddly toy.
As brave as a gladiator, as warm as a fire.
A smile as big as the moon.
As sweet as chocolate.
Bushes instead of eyebrows, with just a blanket
Of snow behind the ears.
Yes that's him, that's my loveable grandad,
He makes me feel happy.

Gemma Ford (10)
Blackwood School, Sutton Coldfield

Hullabaloo

H   is for Holly who jumps up and down
U   is for Uncle who owns a new crown
L   is for Lucy who stares and stares
L   is for landlord who paints dragon lairs
A   is for Adam who races around
B   is for beggar who lives on the ground
A   is for Alison who works really hard
L   is for landlady who sends a nice card
O   is for Oliver who likes to do maths
O   is for Olie who likes to sail rafts.

Jacob Wilkins (8)
Blackwood School, Sutton Coldfield

HULLABALOO

H is for Hannah
   who scribbles on the walls
U is for Uncle
   who always falls
L is for Lauren
   who giggles all the time
L is for Lewis
   who eats all the lime
A is for Alison
   who always shows off
B is for Bethany
   who always coughs
A is for Alex
   who always cuts his hair
L is for Louis
   who always is bare
O is for Oliver
   who screams at his mom
O is for Oscar
   who always eats a poppadom.

Melissa Brookes (8)
Blackwood School, Sutton Coldfield

WINTER

Winter is my favourite time of year
When the snow falls on the ground it looks all clean and clear.

Winter is my favourite time of year
All the ice and snow is out here.

Winter is my favourite time of year
When the snow is clean and clear.

Emily Jones (8)
Blackwood School, Sutton Coldfield

CROCODILE TEARS

If you see a crocodile
It is best not to go near
For if you see it crying
Those are fake crocodile tears.

Every time you go near
When the crocodile cries
Its tears will hypnotise
So don't go near its cries.

Yes, crocodiles are sneaky
For they want their dinner
The dinner might be you
If you go near crocodile tears.

Crocodiles, crocodiles!
When do they stop crying?
For if you see a crocodile
You had better start spying!

Sze-Von Lam (8)
Blackwood School, Sutton Coldfield

MY BROTHER IS THE BEST

I have the best brother
Better than any other.

He is so funny
He tickles your tummy.

He loves Power Rangers
And never goes off with strangers.

He is the very best so we should give him
A rest from being a pest!

Kiran Kadara (9)
Blackwood School, Sutton Coldfield

TOMMY AND THE MAGICIAN

The magician tried to pull Tommy out of a hat
Tommy said, 'Enough of that.'

The magician tried to put Tommy into a box and ran a sword through
Tommy said, 'Try something new.'

The magician tried to get Tommy to lie down flat,
'I'm going to saw you in two.'
Tommy said, 'Is that all you could do?'

The magician tried to get Tommy to disappear into thin air
Tommy said, 'You just dare.'

The magician said, 'What will you do?'
Tommy said, 'Goodbye to you.'

Rachel Sheldon (8)
Blackwood School, Sutton Coldfield

HULLABALOO

H is for Hannah who hops down the stairs
U is for Una who washes and combs her hair
L is for Lauren who skips down the hall
L is for Lee who licks lollipops in the pool
A is for Ambley who fights with her brother
B is for Barry who hates playing with others
A is for Andrew who has broken his leg
L is for Laura who collects clothes pegs
O is for Oliver who shouts very loud
O is for Olivia who stands out in the crowd.

Georgia Robinson (9)
Blackwood School, Sutton Coldfield

AUTUMN POEM

In autumn it is dark and damp
When you walk around you might need a lamp
Autumn leaves start to fall down
And they turn different colours like brown.

In autumn it's not very warm
And it goes colder at every crack of dawn
Kicking through the autumn leaves
You can feel the cool breeze.

In autumn the conkers fall
Some just drop and some hit the wall
Autumn is my favourite season
And I have just told you my reason.

Ryan Barley (8)
Blackwood School, Sutton Coldfield

HULLABALOO

H   is for Hannah who is kind and generous
U   is for Uncle who always helps us
L   is for Lauren who giggles and laughs
L   is for Louise who hates taking a bath
A   is for Alison who always thinks about her tum
B   is for Baker who made a delicious bun
A   is for Aimee who screams and shouts
L   is for Laura who plays about
O   is for Oliver who went to the zoo
O   is for Oscar who bounced on a kangaroo.

Jade Wright (8)
Blackwood School, Sutton Coldfield

School Time

S is for school where we go every day
C is for classes where we learn and play
H is for homework which we don't enjoy
O is for Oliver who is a naughty boy
O is for orange a colour we like
L is for lessons which we dislike

T is for teachers who have taught us all we know
I is for infants who still have a long way to go
M is for mathematics where I am quite bright
E is for English where we read and write.

Alison Wright (8)
Blackwood School, Sutton Coldfield

Fantasty Football

Football crazy
Football mad
I've been playing football since I was a little lad.
Football is my life
Football is the best
Many times I've kicked the ball into the net.
I'm always singing about my team
They're at the bottom of the table
Like Jesus in the stable.
I hope he will save us
and do us a favour
To keep us from danger.

Simrun Mander (9)
Blackwood School, Sutton Coldfield

AUTUMN LEAVES

Autumn is the brightest season
Stay still and I'll give you the reason.

Falling leaves from the trees
In the trees hide the bees.

When I go outside I pick up the leaves and they crunch
I have rice crispies for breakfast and I munch.

Can you smell the leaves on the blazing bonfire?
The fire keeps on getting higher.

It's getting bitter outside
So we'd better get in and hide.

It's getting dark early at night
The moon is glimmering very bright.

The leaves are green, golden and red
Sorry, it's time I went to bed!

Dylan Fox (8)
Blackwood School, Sutton Coldfield

HULLABALOO

H   is for Harry who plays out all the time
U   is for Uncle who makes up rhymes
L   is for lolly who is sticky everywhere
L   is for Laura who loves pears
A   is for Adam who is very fussy
B   is for Ben who is a wussy
A   is for Amba who goes to the fair
L   is for Lucy who plays with her hair
O   is for Owen who plays football
O   is for Oliver who plays in the hall.

Emma Brooke (9)
Blackwood School, Sutton Coldfield

ANIMALS, ANIMALS

Rhinos have wrinkly skin
Dolphins have two wet fins.

Gerbils have useful whiskers
Hedgehogs have prickly briskers.

Leopards have scary claws
Lions make loud roars.

Tigers markings are stripes
Pigs feed from tripes.

Ostriches have enormous legs
Hens lay small, round eggs.

Rabbits have two large teeth
Fishes swim about in the reef.

Sloths hang upside down
Baboons always look like they frown.

Tortoises walk very slow
Worms always get eaten by crows.

Giraffes have thin, long necks
Sharks hang about at shipwrecks.

Owls at night never nap
And that is the animal rap.

James Rogers (9)
Blackwood School, Sutton Coldfield

MY CATS

I have a cat called Brian
Another one called Daisy
Sometimes they are playful
But other times they are lazy.

They eat food called Whiskas
And other types like Go-Kat
After they have eaten it
They lie on their mat.

When we go on holiday
The cats are left alone
But they both jump up at me
When we come home.

Brian's birthday is in January
He is fourteen
Daisy's is in July
She is thirteen.

It is good to have two cats
You can have fun twice
They are really, really cute
As well as really, really nice.

Megan Green (9)
Blackwood School, Sutton Coldfield

HULLABALOO

H   is for Harriet
    who sets up the crime.
U   is for Uncle
    who walks fine
L   is for Laura
    who looks at the stars
L   is for Lucy
    who went to Mars
A   is for Adam
    who likes glue
B   is for Barry
    who has got the flu
A   is for Andrew
    who loves school
L   is for Lauren
    who is always a fool
O   is for Oliver
    who likes to play
O   is for Olive
    who's had a good day.

William Bennison (8)
Blackwood School, Sutton Coldfield

THE ROLLER COASTER

Sit in your seat that's tightly locked
On this ride you will be shocked.
Clunk, we're off, right up the hill,
Oh my stomach!
I need a pill.
At the top see the view,
Anymore and I'm going to spew.
Spinning, spinning, round and round
Really high above the ground.
Metal slats making noises,
Little screaming high-pitch voices.
Here we go, loop-the-loop.
Here's the last bend, we've got to stoop.
Back at last to the start,
Clunk, we've stopped
Let's depart.

Chloë McCarty (9)
Blackwood School, Sutton Coldfield

FRIENDSHIP

Friendship is a special gift
Which you can't see or hold
But when you have a true good friend
They're worth their weight in gold.

Friendship is a special feeling
That keeps you safe and warm
Like the way you feel
When you reach home after a storm.

Laura Clark (9)
Blackwood School, Sutton Coldfield

SNOWY DAY TODAY

Today
The snow came down really fast
Floating feathers of frost.

Today
The snow is white and sparkly
Covering the ground with white snow.

Today
The snow is still here but
Slowly going away.

Today
We're going to make the most of it
Knowing that it won't last.

Hannah Deakin (9)
Blackwood School, Sutton Coldfield

HULLABALOO

H   is for Hound who howls all night
U   is for Uncle who fights with might
L   is for Laura who is horrible
L   is for Luke who is terrible
A   is for Alison who is smart
B   is for Bart who threw a dart
A   is for Andy who drinks like a fish
L   is for Lulu who just wants a wish
O   is for Oliver who is a good friend
O   is for O'Mally who brings my poem to the end.

James Smith (9)
Blackwood School, Sutton Coldfield

HULLABALOO

H is for Henry,
   who never gets a penny
U is for Uncle
   who hunts for wood but never gets many
L is for Laura
   who knows her maths
L is for Lianna,
   who goes somewhere else but never knows the paths
A is for Andrew
   who goes on TV live
B is for Ben
   who owns a beehive
A is for Anna
   who owns a shop
L is for Larry
   who won a year's supply of pop
O is for Oliver
   who plays with his favourite toy
O is for Owen
   who wants to buy a Game Boy.

Andrew Smith (8)
Blackwood School, Sutton Coldfield

HULLABALOO

H is for Harold
    who eats all the time
U is for Uncle
    who causes some crime
L is for Lara
    who has got a friend called Tara
L is for Laura
    who likes crafty Martha
A is for Andrew
    who keeps on saying, 'Hey Yo'
B is for Bert
    who loves black fuzzy crows
A is for Amy
    who always wears nice clothes
L is for Luke
    who is always biting his toes
O is for Ollie
    who likes to eat a red lolly
O is for Olivia
    who has broken her tibia.

Sarah Arrowsmith (8)
Blackwood School, Sutton Coldfield

HULLABALOO

H   is for Hagrid
   who sits on the floor
U   is for Uncle
   who plays with the door
L   is for Laura
   who plays with Jade's hair
L   is for Lewis
   who eats his pear
A   is for Alex
   who plays with his coat
B   is for baby
   who takes a ride on a boat
A   is for Alison
   who makes lots of noise
L   is for Lotty
   who plays with her toys
O   is for Oliver
   who splashes in the puddle
O   is for Olivia
   who gets in a muddle.

Lauren Langdell (8)
Blackwood School, Sutton Coldfield

SEASONS

I like the spring feeling
And the summer too
I put my red shorts on and my T-shirt that's blue
I also wear my swimsuit with a polka dot or two
The paddling pool is ready for me to jump right in
I look into the water and suddenly see a fin
It must be my goldfish that has jumped out of his skin
So I will have to rescue him before it is too late
Because the local cat thinks he is the bait
I fill the tank with water and put him right back in
I tell him no more adventures as summer is drawing in
I love the autumn morning
And the winter nights
But most of all I love the summer light nights.

Katie Fahey (10)
Blackwood School, Sutton Coldfield

HAPPINESS

I wake up every morning,
And look to greet the sun,
I feel so very happy,
For a new day has begun.
I try to do a good turn,
For someone every day,
And learn to be considerate,
In learning and in play.
So let us pull together,
For kindness we can send,
To everyone we meet each day,
Our family and our friends.

Rebecca Fisher (10)
Blackwood School, Sutton Coldfield

A Theme Park!

Fast rides,
Water rides,
Slow rides,
Baby rides.

Sticky drinks,
Hot drinks,
Fizzy drinks,
Flavoured drinks.

Big hot dogs,
Small hot dogs,
Jumbo hot dogs,
Red sauce hot dogs.

Tall people,
Small people,
Young people,
Old people.

So how about coming to my
Theme park?

Nicola Aston (10)
Blackwood School, Sutton Coldfield

WINTER DAYS

A layer of snow,
covers the ground.
Wrapped up so warm,
slipping around.

Making snowmen,
is quite fun,
although it leaves
your fingers numb.

Snow is falling
trees are bare.
It may be cold
but I don't care.

Charlotte Mead (11)
Blackwood School, Sutton Coldfield

WHY WAR?

Guns banging
Missiles clanging
People screaming
If only I was dreaming.

People dying
Children crying
Soldiers running
The enemy is coming.

People shot
Lives gone to pot.

Russell Melville (10)
Blackwood School, Sutton Coldfield

LUNCHTIME

It's lunchtime,
It's lunchtime,
It's time to munch time
Everyone in a bunch time.

What shall I eat today?
How much will I have to pay?
Not too much, not too little
Where shall I sit? I will sit in the middle.

Go back out to play, oh no it's raining,
The dinnerladies are complaining,
Go back in because now it's hailing,
That'll start the teacher wailing.

Claire Andrews (10)
Blackwood School, Sutton Coldfield

NETBALL

Netball is my game
And Lucie is my name,
I like to play as goal attack
And when I score I never look back.

There are three sections to our court
But all the boys think it is such a rubbish sport
I have never missed a catch
And we have never lost a match.

Our team colour is green
And I am so fast I can't be seen
I whiz up and down the court,
Yes! Netball really is my sport.

Lucie Irving (11)
Blackwood School, Sutton Coldfield

PLEASE MR MEAKIN
(Based on 'Please Mrs Butler' by Allan Ahlberg)

'Please Mr Meakin,
This boy Mark Drew,
Keeps taking my ruler, Sir
What shall I do?'

'Hide it in your drawer dear,
Put it in the sink,
Snap it if you want my baby
Do whatever you think.'

'Please Mr Meakin,
This boy Mark Drew,
Keeps calling me nasty names, Sir,
What shall I do?'

'Run away to France dear,
Smack him if he is a pest,
Go on top of the roof my flower,
Do what you think's best.'

'Please Mr Meakin,
This boy Mark Drew,
Keeps copying my picture, Sir
What shall I do?'

'Hide it in the staffroom dear,
Go to London Zoo,
Tickle him if you want my lamb,
Do what you want to do.'

Ben Jones (8)
Blackwood School, Sutton Coldfield

A COUNTING POEM

Ten little children
All drinking wine
One got very drunk
And then there were nine.

Nine little children
All lifting weights
One dropped it on his toes
And then there were eight.

Eight little children
Floating up to Heaven
Then came an aeroplane
And then there were seven.

Seven little children
All mixing a mix
One lost its arm
And then there were six.

Six little children
All prodding beehives
One got stung
And then there were five.

Five little children
All eating sweets
One shouted more, and broke his jaw
And then there were four.

Four little children
Cutting down the trees
One fell on top of him
And then there were three.

Three little children
All saying moo
One turned into a cow
And then there were two.

Two little children
Both having fun
One slipped over
And then there was one.

One little child
Doing magic, called John
He got it all wrong
And then there were none.

Alice Keen (7)
Blackwood School, Sutton Coldfield

LUNCHTIME

Lunchtime, lunchtime, lunchtime,
We sit down with our friends,
Our food crunches and it's munchtime
At 12.30pm our munchtime ends.

At wet lunchtime we stay in
We play a game or with the blocks
Outside it is pouring with rain
When it's pouring, people are trying to get in
But the door is locked.

When we go outside to play with our friends
We play a good fun game,
When the whistle blows, playtime ends,
When we come in, I think work is a right pain.

Amberley Fisher (10)
Blackwood School, Sutton Coldfield

DAYTIME

Flowers and trees in the morning breeze
The sky a shade of blue.
The sun shining on the trees,
And the morning dew.

The birds sing and care for their young,
The frogs look after their spawn.
I will play and play this very day
Until it comes to dawn.

When night comes I will run inside
And drink tea by the fire,
Jessy comes and sits with me
For she is my desire.

Now I'm going off to bed
And that's where I shall stay,
Until I can go outside,
The very next day.

Livvy Callaghan (10)
Blackwood School, Sutton Coldfield

HAVING FUN REALLY IS COOL

Sleepovers, parties and hot summer days,
Trampolining, dancing and happy holidays.
Swimming, singing, and playing with friends,
Board games, computers, the fun never ends.

Christmas, birthdays, and baking a cake,
Colouring, drawing and finding something to make.
Laughing, joking and playing the fool,
Being young, having fun, really is cool.

Charlotte Harrison (10)
Blackwood School, Sutton Coldfield

MY IMAGINARY THEME PARK

My theme park
Would have to be
One with
Happy families.

The Hubba Pubba
The Ringy Ting
Lots of rides
Are all my thing.

Loads of kids
Want to go
Pretty children
With a bow.

The pirate ship
Come with me,
This wonderful ship
You have to see.

The log flume
Zoom, splash,
The bumper cars
Boom, crash.

Oh no,
It's my mum
See you later
I've got to fill my tum!

Emma Longmore (10)
Blackwood School, Sutton Coldfield

GRANDAD

His special chair
He calls it,
His favourite place of all.
Sits there telling stories
of his past.
When I run into his house
he gives me an enormous hug,
throws me in the air.
He teases me saying I love my other grandad more.
His bald haircut is snow
with his foggy eyes that match.
I sit in the chair for hours
thinking about his past.
His voice is squeaky.
He says he's as quick as a fox
but he's . . .
as slow as a tortoise.
Years and years have passed by,
he's still sitting in the same old chair.

Sasha Sokhal (9)
Blackwood School, Sutton Coldfield

AN ORDINARY LUNCHTIME AT BLACKWOOD SCHOOL

I lunged into the classroom, Greg and Loveen had saved me a seat.
I crept around the dinner ladies that I didn't want to meet.
Crash! Spill! Crunch!

Miss Stop-Doing-That roared,
'How did you spill your drink?'
Munching crisps I explained to her
That I'd taken a nasty dip in the sink.
Splurge! Scream! Bang!

Marking maths books madly
Mrs Detention looked like she was going insane
Looking at me badly
Like the impact of a cane
Over the noise of a girl slurping
And the sound of dirty boys burping
I heard the nasty grumble of my name.
Cross! Wrong! Cross!

In burst the head teacher
With a nasty look on her face
I'm sure that she noticed
That the room was a disgrace.
Thump! Bump! Smack!

'I'll sack every teacher, I'll expel every kid,
What a huge feature, I'll make a few quid.
I'm sure I won't be breaking a rule'
And that was just a normal lunchtime at Blackwood School.

Ross Higgins (10)
Blackwood School, Sutton Coldfield

ONE-MAN BAND

My body is a one-man band,
I hear rhythm when I clap my hand.

Even when I stamp my feet,
I find I make a groovy beat.

Strangely when I blow my nose,
It sounds like a trumpet, I suppose.

If I mumble in a space,
It echoes like a double bass.

My hiccups after a meal
Remind me of a glockenspiel.

Deep low rumbles in my tum,
Sound very like a big bass drum.

My voice can reach notes high and low,
From a tuba to a piccolo.

So if all the children formed a band,
We'd all be heard throughout the land.

Stuart Purser (10)
Blackwood School, Sutton Coldfield

CELEBRATIONS

Sweets and chocolates are so yummy,
They will fill my big fat tummy.

Enormous presents make me happy
My baby cousin will fill his nappy.

Music is so groovy,
Are you having a Christmas boogie?

Santa is coming at 12 o'clock
but he doesn't go *knock, knock.*

Christmas trees are so pretty
Have you got one? *No?* That's a pity.

At Christmas time there's no school
And I think that's so cool.

Crackers are part of Christmas fun,
Even though the gifts are dumb.

Christmas cake and cream is sweet and runny
Just like a dollop of sweet, sweet honey.

Jonathan Barakât (9)
Blackwood School, Sutton Coldfield

LUNCHTIME

Yahoo, hooray!
The bell has gone, it's dinner time again,
We stack our books,
Move our chairs,
And run out through the door.

Back in Mrs Perry's room, eating all our lunch,
And Mrs Baxter saying we're a rowdy bunch,
And Joe gives Kieran a punch.

It was snowing today,
Yahoo, hooray!
I wanted to play in the snow,
I had snow in my hair,
But it was so unfair,
When the teacher came out to say,
'You can't stay out and play today in the snow,
It's much too cold.'
So we did as we were told.

James Waters (9)
Blackwood School, Sutton Coldfield

LUNCHTIME

It's another lunchtime I'm feeling rather glum,
I'm eating in Mrs Perry's room it's sure to be good fun.
Mrs Baxter is blowing her head off once again
And Zoë Spence is trying to remove another chocolate stain.

The gang in the corner are messing around
They throw Walkers crisps at me but as they hit the ground,
Mrs Perry shouts at them and blows their heads off high
Mrs Baxter comes over and gives a big sigh.

Crash, bang, wallop, there goes a lunch box all over the floor
Then Mrs Cocken comes knocking on our door.
'What's going on in here?' that's what she said
'It's all big Bert's fault,' said little Ned.

I want to stay out of that row,
I'd better leave this room right now
As I put my lunch away
I think of a better lunch than today.

Laura Steventon (10)
Blackwood School, Sutton Coldfield

CRAZY LUNCHTIME

I talk to my friend
I think about going home
I hear dinner lady shouting
Girls screaming
I hear crunching and popping
Chairs squeaking
Flying sandwiches
People banging tables
Boy shouting loudly
Drink slurping
Chocolate cakes jumping
Boy running madly
Girls chatting
Boys burping
Girls drinking
Dinner ladies going red
Boys shouting
And the bell rings for lessons.

Georgia Cash (9)
Blackwood School, Sutton Coldfield

FUNFAIR

It's Saturday morning the sun is blazing
I think today is going to be amazing
Because we are going to the funfair.

We get in the car ready to go
Travelling at three miles per hour really slow
We arrive at the fair just in time
To go on a ride called Scary Skeleton ride.

After that we go on the big slide
Where my little sister gets scared and cries
Then we go and get some lunch
I have a packet of crisps and some grapes in a bunch.

Then we watch the dog show
But unfortunately after that we have to go
But before we go we get some ice cream
But my sister hates them so she shouts and screams
So we go and get her a lollipop
Which she dribbles all down her top.

So we go back to the car
And we haven't travelled far
When my sister falls fast asleep
At last peace, not a single peep.

Nicola Pitt (10)
Blackwood School, Sutton Coldfield

LUNCHTIME

Lunchtimes can be a terrible time,
There is noise and clatter, laughter and chatter.

Lunchtimes can be a terrible time
With lunches splatted on the floor,
People start to slip and slide,
Lunchtimes can be a terrible time.

'Five minutes to go,' shouts Mrs Baxter
Lunchtimes can be a terrible time.

Yogurts spilt, baybells fly,
Tomatoes squashed and bananas . . . bye-bye!
Lunchtimes can be a terrible time,
Yum, yum, yum, hardly anything going in my tum, tum, tum.

Brriiinnnngg! Lunchtime is over
Lunchtimes can be a terrible time
. . . but only sometimes.

Matthew Walker (10)
Blackwood School, Sutton Coldfield

DISASTROUS DINNER TIME!

On each day of the week,
We sit down and hear the chairs squeak.
With salty crisps and sticky jam,
Both in the lunch box of a girl named Pam.

Peanut butter, cakes and bread,
The dinner lady shakes her head.
Everyone rushes to grab a seat
Oh no, Ben has tripped over his feet.
I have a munch,
And my sandwich goes crunch.
Tim Tunnel keeps asking for more,
His friends give it him and it ends up on the floor.

The dinner lady shakes her head,
Those naughty kids are messing about,
She's had enough and there's no doubt
No doubt, no doubt, the dinner lady's had enough
And there's no doubt.

With naughty Fred Find, throwing food to the wall,
Bad tempered Ann got annoyed
And grabbed his bouncy ball.
I finished my crisps, my friends did too,
We hurried up as we needed the loo.
Look, come on, it's time to play,
As lunch is over for another day.

Natasha Bodenham (10)
Blackwood School, Sutton Coldfield

DISASTROUS DINNER TIME

I grab my lunch box and sit down,
I take a peek inside, I start to
Munch my sandwich and notice a box,
I hadn't put it inside.
I take off the lid . . .
Health food!
It's in the bin, OK.

Suddenly my friend comes past,
And knocks over my drink
Over the floor, and on my skirt,
Plus the table *drip . . . drip . . . drip,*
I run to the sink to clean my skirt.

I go back to the table and start
To laugh and joke, and suddenly,
Find my last piece soaked
Oh no!

Oh I really hate lunchtimes
I really, really do.
I hope lunch is better
Or I'll end up bending
Over the loo.

Hannah Shaw **(9)**
Blackwood School, Sutton Coldfield

SADNESS IS . . .

Sadness is
Not having any chocolates
Sadness is
Being lonely in a nasty way
Sadness is
Having bad weather
Sadness is
Not having any friends
Sadness is
Having a big brother and sister
Sadness is
Losing football matches
Sadness is
Having an unlucky day
Sadness is
Being hurt by words.

Loveen Dyall (9)
Blackwood School, Sutton Coldfield

HAPPY HOLIDAY

S   is for seagulls you find in the sky
T   is for tiny fishes swimming free
A   is for anchors which lie on the sand
R   is for rock pools with creatures inside
F   is for fishes which swim in the sea
I   is for ice cream running down my throat
S   is for surfers who surf on the waves
H   is for happiness on holidays!

Abigail Lamond (9)
Blackwood School, Sutton Coldfield

LEAVES

When the wind goes past the trees,
It takes them off and away like thieves,
High, high, high above,
As high as an eagle as high as a dove,
Down,
  Down,
    Down,
      Down,
        Back again on the green grass,
To be trod on and not be seen.
When kites fly and dive to the ground,
It makes the leaves spin round and round,
And that's my poem about leaves,
And how the wind takes them off the trees,
And how the wind takes them like thieves.

Grace Carrington (10)
Blackwood School, Sutton Coldfield

WHAT IS YELLOW?

What is yellow?
Yellow is creamy,
Bright and sunny,
Nice and dreamy,
Yellow is the sun,
The birds and the fish,
Yellow is the colour that makes a tasty dish.
Yellow is soft,
Yellow is kind,
Yellow is the colour of happiness inside.

Jessica Lear (11)
Blackwood School, Sutton Coldfield

LUNCHTIME BLUES

I rush to get a seat,
All I do is eat,
Crisp bags rattling,
Knives and forks clattering,
Oh, the lunchtime blues.

Yucky yoghurts, slivery sandwiches,
'What have you got for dinner?' I say.
'Let's go out to play, hooray, hooray.'
Oh, the lunchtime blues.

Children shouting so, so loud,
Everybody is grumpy, because the field's out of bound,
Oh, the lunchtime blues.

Dinner ladies shrieking,
Lots of children speaking,
The dinner lady said, 'Shut up.'
Oh, the lunchtime blues.

Chloe Bates (10)
Blackwood School, Sutton Coldfield

IT'S DINNER TIME

The bell goes, hooray! it's dinnertime,
Yack what juice you got? I think it's lime.
Crisp packets go *bang*
Drinks and bottles go *clang*.
It's dinner time, dinner time, hooray.

Yucky yoghurts slide,
Across the table sandwiches glide.
Children shouting at the top of their voices,
There are so many different noises.
It's dinner time, dinner time, hooray.

At the table, the boys are all joking,
And in the corner, two children poking.
Soggy sandwiches slip to the floor,
And some even get kicked under the door.
It's dinner time, dinner time, hooray.

Lunch boxes can be such fun,
If they contain a big iced bun.
But sometimes inside there's a piece of old fruit,
Squashed in a corner not looking so cute.
It's dinner time, dinner time, hooray.

Packets of crisps go *crunch, crunch,*
As everybody eats their yuckety lunch.
Some of the dinner ladies start to squeal,
And before you know it we all took to heal.
It's dinner time, dinner time, hooray.

If lunchtime was quiet and reasonably calm,
And if there was nothing to cause us alarm.
I think I'd really enjoy lunchtime,
And still be able to make my poem rhyme.
Lunch is over, lunch is over, hooray, hooray.

Danielle Duggan (10)
Blackwood School, Sutton Coldfield

My Dream Theme Park

My dream theme park would be
Filled with happiness and glee
Animals, rides and clowns too
A place where the sun always shines
And the sky is always blue.
I would like all the rides to be free
Why don't you come and see?
If you are in the mood
You might fancy some food.
Pizzas, hot dogs and fish and chips
The sauce will get to your fingertips
You can go on the roller coaster
Or you could have a free poster.

Joanne Shepherd (10)
Blackwood School, Sutton Coldfield

Snowmen

Snowmen are made out of snow
Snowmen are soggy and wet
Snowmen don't last very long
Snowmen sit on snow walls
Snowmen are round and fat
Snowmen melt when it rains and the sun shines
Snowmen are cold and big
Snowmen wear hats and scarves
Snowmen shine so bright
Snowmen are the best.

Jade Hitchcock (8)
Colley Lane Primary School, Halesowen

DREAMLAND

D olphins were in a swimming pool
so once again I can swim with them
R oller was one of my dolphins and
jumps when I am on her back
E melia is my sister's dolphin
so she can do the same stuff as me
A dventures we can do in the water
to the bottom high in the sky
M y favourite is Pongo she is the fastest
in the water and jumps so quick
L ife was not as nice sometimes
because they splash at me
A musement is what I like from them
but sometimes they do not give me amusement
N utty but nice they are
sometimes perfect for me
D reams will not always come true
but this is not going to come true.

Bryony Crumpton (8)
Colley Lane Primary School, Halesowen

MY DREAM

M y dream is about being on holiday
Y es an imaginary holiday.

D olphins, sharks, fish,
R aging sharks rampage round the sea
E lectric eels give you quite a shock
A ll the fish fill the sea
M ountains of creatures I see round the sea.

Daniel Crowe (9)
Colley Lane Primary School, Halesowen

MAN UTD

F   ans are going crazy
O   nly the keeper to beat
O   ne-nil to United
T   he ball's in the back of the net
B   arthez saves a penalty kick
A   nother ten minutes to go
L   ong ball finds van Nistelrooy
L   obs the goalie now it's two.

T   he ref blows the final whistle
E   veryone cheers in the ground
A   nother win for Ferguson
M   an United the best team around.

James Taylor (8)
Colley Lane Primary School, Halesowen

MY ROOM

My room most people keep out
It runs right against the chimney spout.

I have a city built of Lego
To my little brother I say go.

I enjoy my room
It's like a home to me
If you enter in you'll go boom!
Just wait and see.

Daniel Parsons (8)
Colley Lane Primary School, Halesowen

MY CAT

My cat dances
My cat prances
She lets me tickle her tummy
And she's very, very funny.

My cat's called Milly
My cat's silly
She looks in the window just to see,
If I am in because she loves me!

Amy Blount (9)
Colley Lane Primary School, Halesowen

CHRISTMAS DAY

Santa slow, Santa show
Santa sees naughty snow.
People sledging sliding scared
Scattering snow flows in the air.
So snowy snow
So skies squeal
Squeaky peeling skies.

Gameel Maged (8)
Colley Lane Primary School, Halesowen

MY FAVOURITE ANIMAL

It's time for my cat to have her food
But she says she's not in the mood
She always miaows like the foxes howl
But we never care
Because she's always there to share.

Hannah Smallpage-Hurst (8)
Colley Lane Primary School, Halesowen

CLOUD NINE

Cloud Nine is like you are floating in candy
I would like to, I would like to be on a cloud.
It's like you're in a candy stick in your brain,
And on each and everyone of them there is a hand.
I like the chocolate land the best,
But if you want a taxi you can't have one
Because I eat them all up.

Elizabeth Dear (9)
Colley Lane Primary School, Halesowen

MY ROOM

M agazines I read when I go to bed
Y ummy sweets me and my friend eat

R ubbish in the bin in my room
O bjects all around my bedroom
O dd pairs of socks in my drawer
M om might shut my door on a night.

Charlie Carrington (9)
Colley Lane Primary School, Halesowen

PETS

P ets are fun, pets are cool
E verywhere you go pets are there
T here is one now in front of you
S o pick it up and keep it.

Derrie Pearson (9)
Colley Lane Primary School, Halesowen

FRIENDS

F is for friendship
R is for relationship
I   is for intelligent
E is forever best friends
N is for nice
D is for dopey
S is for special friends.

Tammie Foster (8)
Colley Lane Primary School, Halesowen

ASHLEY

A shley is very sweet
S he can sometimes be neat
H her hair is thin
L ives a luxury life
E asily seen
Y our house is not clean.

Holly Harvey (9)
Colley Lane Primary School, Halesowen

FEARS

F ire is the first fear
E arthquakes make my house shake
A nts, red ants that bite you
R ats and mice, they smell bad
S piders with their long, eight, hairy legs.

Stacie Hingley (9)
Colley Lane Primary School, Halesowen

BE AFRAID, BE VERY AFRAID

G hosts and ghouls surround you
R IP to you the reader
A nything you do don't wake the dead
V ery gruesome deaths
E very zombie you kill, they come to life
Y ou be very aware
A nything you do don't touch a thing
R ight you are not safe
D on't run you can't get out.

Sam Resuggan (9)
Colley Lane Primary School, Halesowen

MY ROOM

M y room is so messy
Y uk! The smell is disgusting

R ubbish all over the floor
O dd books everywhere
O bjects knocked over on the beds and bookshelf
M ates, don't let them in.

Bethany Turner (8)
Colley Lane Primary School, Halesowen

MY PETS

My little, tiny cat's swect and fat
Eating away every single day
She even likes my dad, but I think he is mad.
Her brother's name is Jar Jar he sleeps on the bonnet of the car.
They like to hide in the garden outside.

Jessica Bird (10)
Dingle Community Primary School, Kingswinford

PETS

My pet is a dog
He is called Archy
He picks up my dad's slippers
When people come in
He always jumps up people.

When we are having breakfast
he pushes your leg.
He always creeps up my nan's garden
and headbutts the door.
When we get up on a morning,
he always sleeps on our rug.
He doesn't normally bite things,
but he was biting a hole in the rug.

He loves biscuits like me.

Bradley Ghent (10)
Dingle Community Primary School, Kingswinford

MY PET

My cat is black and white
She always curls up tight
She never goes to bed at night
She pretends to play fight
She never bites.

Her name is Bella
We all really love her
Because she's clever.

She's got a lot of toys
She always makes a purring noise.

Sarah-Jayne Garbett (10)
Dingle Community Primary School, Kingswinford

THE TWO DOGS

I have two dogs
That chased two frogs
They chased them out of town
Wearing my mom's dressing gown.

They chased them into the wood,
Up to Mr Robin Hood.
Then into a cave,
They were pretty brave,
Cos a bear came out
And gave them a clout.

They ran and ran to the countryside,
Now it's time for the dog to hide,
Cos the frogs went down to the river,
And in a flash the frogs were gone
And the dogs were eating liver.

Claire Farmer (10)
Dingle Community Primary School, Kingswinford

PETS

My cat's black and white, he likes to play games
and he smells like bubble bath.

My cat is funny, he makes me laugh
and his favourite food is turkey.

My cat is crazy and he is never lazy.

My cat is cute to care for.

My cat is called Mog and he sits on a log.

Hannah Penn (10)
Dingle Community Primary School, Kingswinford

JOEY

J oey is my little bird, he is quite sweet
and he has little feet.
O n his perch he sits all day
when he's out he likes to play
E very single day
he flies around and then we put him away
Y ou will never find a bird like my Joey.

Amy Smith (10)
Dingle Community Primary School, Kingswinford

ANIMALS

A n antelope is fast.
N ewts are small and they live in hot places.
I nsects are small and some sting and some sneak about.
M onkeys swing from tree to tree to get food.
A lligators have big sharp teeth and are dark green.
L ions are big and they have teeth like claws.
S nakes are sneaky and they slither.

Rachael Platt (10)
Dingle Community Primary School, Kingswinford

MY HORSE, SPLASH

Splash,
Horses are sweet.

With hooves at their feet
If a fly lands on Splash
Splash whacks it in a flash!

Jemima Winwood (10)
Dingle Community Primary School, Kingswinford

ENVIRONMENT

E   nvironment is coming to extinction
N   aughty businessmen are knocking down forests
V   icious, cruel, chopping men
I   n the woods where the animals be, then *bang!* One's dead!
R   abbits are being shot
O   nly the Government can stop them now
N   aughty men
M   en are going to pay for this
E   ngines roar when they knock down trees
N   ow businessmen don't send in your woodchopping men
T   rees are being killed.

Robert Mutch (10)
Dingle Community Primary School, Kingswinford

PETS

My dog, Whisky, is very bright
Just like Ian Wright.
He is the best at jumping,
Especially up people.
He likes bits of fuss and he loves my grandad.
When we go to bed, he sleeps on the landing
And snores loudly.
When we have Sunday dinner, he likes to watch TV.
When we take him on a walk he likes to play with his friends
Called Wisky, Sam, Polly and Whiney.

Zak Westwood (10)
Dingle Community Primary School, Kingswinford

PETS

My pet is called Eva
She is a dog
My dog is female
Her fur is as white as the bark on a tree.

I love my dog.

She eats a lot and a lot
And has not a single spot.
When she was a pup
She broke a cup
She's eighty-four
She can open a door.

Joshua Rock (10)
Dingle Community Primary School, Kingswinford

SHE'S ALL MINE

She's as soft as a new grown dizzy
As fat as a pregnant cow
She runs like the storm blowing wind
Lots of people go wow!
But she can be as careful as a cat
She's gold and white
Just the way I like her
Yes her name is Summer
And sometimes she's a bummer
Of course she's a horse
And I wouldn't trade her for anything.

Alison Starkey (9)
Dingle Community Primary School, Kingswinford

MY PET

My pet has been around for some time,
and it's quite an old one.
In our years she is now twelve
but in their years, eighty-four, now that's old.

Her name is Eva,
and you know she is a girl,
her favourite food is dog biscuits in gravy
her colour is white on the body and brown on the head.

She has done a lot of funny things in the past,
like when she sat down and dragged her bum across
the floor leaving a brown mark,
and if you think that's bad enough,
when we went down the common she got her head
stuck in a tree,
she is house and car trained which comes in handy sometimes.

Daniel Rock (10)
Dingle Community Primary School, Kingswinford

PETS

My cats are black and white and they smell like French bread,
And they're as tough as lead.

My cats are funny and their favourite food is honey.

My cats are lazy and they love to go crazy.

My cats are loving and they are there for my living.

Abby Jones (10)
Dingle Community Primary School, Kingswinford

PETS

My pet is called Monty,
he is a very calm dog,
he likes every visitor,
every time they come,
he always gets excited.

He is a very good dog.

He is an expert at basketball
and he is not very tall,
he is the best dog I will ever have
I hope I am his best friend.

He is a very good dog.

He doesn't eat a lot,
and doesn't have a single spot,
he is fifty-four
and he is able to open a door.

He is a very, very good dog.

I have a new puppy dog,
and she is called Jazz.

Jordan Danks (9)
Dingle Community Primary School, Kingswinford

PETS

My dog is brown and white
She always loves to bite
She lies by the fire
She's a very big liar
My dog is called Kim
She has also got friends called Jim and Tim.

Rebekah Garbett (10)
Dingle Community Primary School, Kingswinford

RABBITS

Rabbits have ears that lop,
rabbits have ears that flop.
They have twitchy noses,
and look as good as roses.
You get some white,
and some as black as night.

Rabbits live in burrows
and run along the furrows.
They sometimes eat clover,
and love the cliffs of Dover.

They jump really high,
they can almost touch the sky.
They can be very quiet,
when we're out they have a riot.

Some rabbits are bad,
some rabbits are mad,
some rabbits are good,
others chew on wood.

Sarah Potter (9)
Dingle Community Primary School, Kingswinford

BLOSSOM

B   lossom is my dog she is . . .
L   oving and friendly
O   ver you and always playful
S   he cheers you up when you're sad
S   he always is cheerful and happy
O   h enjoys playing with you
M   y dog is the best dog in the world.

Andrew Rogerson (9)
Dingle Community Primary School, Kingswinford

PETS

My pet is soft but nice,
He eats snow and chews on ice.
He's brown and white,
But be careful because he can bite.
My pet is called Charlie.
He is funny because he can chase a bunny.
My dog is thirteen.

Once my dog went in the bath
Then he splashed my mum and dad.
When you're finished in the bath or shower,
He drinks the water and smells like a flower.
When my dog is in the garden he gets stuck
In the trees and grazes my knees.
When my dog is in the park he goes down the slide.

Do I like my dog? Of course but you can't be forced.
Out of nowhere he comes like a menace.
Got a dog, you should have because they're playful
And friendly and could be called Dennis.

Thomas Nicholson (9)
Dingle Community Primary School, Kingswinford

THE WIGGLY LITTLE SNAKE

A wiggly snake slithering up the stairs
Slithering on the landing
Slithering on the chairs
Wiggly in the bedroom
Having a sip at the toilet,
Watch out little snake, you're going to get *flushed!*

Joseph Haden (9)
Dingle Community Primary School, Kingswinford

CHARLIE CHOPPER

Before he strikes he waits
He waits for his scrumptious bite,
Its tail moves in an authentic way,
When it's mysterious, it sways and sways,
Its eyes glisten making you swirl,
Swirl and twirl,
Its fluffy ears are soft and smooth,
'Do you know it has a jaggedy tooth?'
Its fur is scruffy and sticks up,
It loves climbing out of a cup,
When I hug it goes a quiver,
When he comes from outside,
Its nickname is Shiver,
When he goes to bed he snores
You can see his sharp, pointy claws,
When it's eating, munching his cat food,
Maybe crunching,
It licks his milk while tearing his quilt.

Sophia Dimopaulou (9)
Dingle Community Primary School, Kingswinford

PETS

My pet is a dog called Tim,
He is funny because he licks your chin.
He isn't old, he's barely one,
If you race him he's already gone.
He can chew anything you say,
He chewed my mom's broom in May.
Tim is a little menace with brooms,
I saw him tearing up shoes.

Elliot Westwood (9)
Dingle Community Primary School, Kingswinford

THE CAT

The cat lies still near the fire
And goes to sleep.
She wakes up
And shuffles to her dinner.
She leaps out to play at night-time
She runs back to her tea
And back to bed near the fire.

Daniel Fellows (9)
Dingle Community Primary School, Kingswinford

THE KILLING WHIPPET

It moves like a cheetah
It kills like a cheetah
It feels very, very rough
And it smells like rotten egg that wakes the dead.
And it looks like a human dart spitting through the night.
Watch out, it will get you soon and rip your tender skin out.

Daniel Lamb (9)
Dingle Community Primary School, Kingswinford

ANIMAL MIX

A jealous dog looking for a frog
A big fat rat looking for a rat
A big fat rat creeping up a cat's back
A big fat cat preying to kill a rat.

Kieran Bates (8)
Dingle Community Primary School, Kingswinford

LAND RUNNER

A clawed beast
A chicken killer
The land runner
One look or smell, you're gone
Rabbit killer
Always ready with gnashing teeth
To rip its prey
As fast as lightning
A man's best friend but still a killer
The speed it runs it could be an Olympic runner
Furry animal, but don't be fooled
They're still killers.

Benjamin Jones (9)
Dingle Community Primary School, Kingswinford

THE ANIMAL CALLED PIP

I have a funny pet
The animal is a hamster, it is called Pip.
Sometimes she's fast as she crawls along the ground,
She crawls like mad.
Maybe she will bite, she might not.
But if you're kind, she won't.
If you keep calm, she will not hurt, OK?
Of course she likes to be in her ball!
When she looks out of her cage, if she sees a cat
She will go mad!

Emily Fisher (9)
Dingle Community Primary School, Kingswinford

CLEVER CAT

A brown tabby cat is hiding around the brick wall
As it's placing each paw carefully not putting a paw wrong.
It is in the position to strike at a lost mouse,
The cat stays still as a statue.
It pounces on the mouse.
It kills the lost mouse.
When it is done, it licks its paws
And walks away proudly.

Rachel Wood (9)
Dingle Community Primary School, Kingswinford

JAKE

J   ake
A   very good joker
K   icks me under the table
E   asy to catch outside.

Sarina Lad (8)
Dingle Community Primary School, Kingswinford

JAMES

J   ames
A   normal boy with pointy hair
M   ean to his brother
E   ven at home
S   ometimes he is weird!

Kimberley Fennell (8)
Dingle Community Primary School, Kingswinford

THE CREEPY SPIDER

On its hairy legs, it creeps slowly from cobweb to cobweb
Looking for prey,
It's eight long legs, step forward,
Its eyes glow like emeralds, his body is triangular with stick up hairs,
I'm watching it poised to grab a tiny fly.
It's waiting patiently to jump,
Then suddenly,
I see no fly just a tiny grin off one big spider.

Christopher Round (9)
Dingle Community Primary School, Kingswinford

THOMAS

T   homas
H   as a cool hairstyle
O   n Sunday he plays a match and
M   akes the goals
A   nd sometimes he scores a cracker
S   ome of them set him up.

James Baxter (8)
Dingle Community Primary School, Kingswinford

CHLOE

C   hloe
H   as glossy blue eyes
L   istens very well
O   n the tables she is very helpful
E   ntertains people when they are sad.

Jodi Cooper (8)
Dingle Community Primary School, Kingswinford

MOLLY THE CAT

She's thin and silky smooth,
When you stroke her kindly,
She brushes her tail across your leg,
She will take good care of you,
She will love you too.
Molly will talk to you if she is hungry or sad.
Molly will treat you like a mother,
She will go into the garden to catch her prey,
She walks closer, not putting one foot wrong . . . *Boom!*
She caught her prey, it was a . . .
Butterfly, she will take it to you for a present
To show that she loves you.

Chloe Gillard (9)
Dingle Community Primary School, Kingswinford

WATCH OUT HAMSTER

When the clock strikes six
Out of his burrow comes the white hamster
Hunting for seeds.
The foxes are stirring
Second by second dozier they get.
Run
Run like a volcano
Fear like a fire
Safe
Safe in his burrow
Sleep sweet sleep.

Martin Siviter (9)
Dingle Community Primary School, Kingswinford

A CAT

The cat moves like a hunting lion in the grass
The cat looks like a furry ball rolling down the stairs
It runs up and down like a mad yo-yo
I think it is crazier than a baboon
And then a big dog comes along and scares the poor thing,
The cat went to hospital because the dog hurt the cat badly
The cat went after the dog and then the cat beat up the dog badly
The next day they were all better and made friends.

Amy Davies (8)
Dingle Community Primary School, Kingswinford

THE TABBY CAT

The ginger cat, he feels so soft and slender,
While rubbing his paws against the swaying grass.
How he trots across the solid pavement.
Not a step out of line when you see him pass.
His tail swishing in the blazing sun.
Staring quietly at people as they pass.

Hayley Siviter (9)
Dingle Community Primary School, Kingswinford

GO LITTLE DOGGY

Go little doggy bowl the skittles over
Go little doggy make a massive clover
Go little doggy walk and you'll improve
Go little doggy your fur is so smooth
Go little doggy zoom to the North Pole
Go little doggy and you'll score the *goal!*

Stefanie Ward (8)
Dingle Community Primary School, Kingswinford

THE OCEAN

One night I was lying in my bed
When a marvellous thought came into my head
To sail across the ocean blue
And take my dog Sam too.
First I would need a ship
So I'll go and get wood from the skip.
I'll need to ask my dad for nails
I'll build this ship even if it hails.
I'll make it waterproof so it doesn't sink.
What colour shall I paint it? Let me think.
Oh yes, brown.
I'll need to get the paint from the town.
'Get up, get up'
And all this was a dream.

Rhianna Davies (10)
Dingle Community Primary School, Kingswinford

THE CAT

She creeps along
Not putting a foot wrong,
Her slender legs,
Look like little pegs,
Her fur sticking on end,
Her back legs bend,
Look out mouse,
The cat's in the house.
She gets ready and 'springs'
Upon the little thing
Then gobbles it up.

Cole Hickman (8)
Dingle Community Primary School, Kingswinford

MY LITTLE HUNTING CAT

She moves so tenderly outside, not putting a paw out of place
She sees her victim out the eye,
And a smile spreads over her face.
She gets in the right position for pouncing
Freezes for a minute or two
Then suddenly she jumps out her hiding hole
And in very short notice
Eats up the mouse's poor little soul.

Chloe Rutherford (8)
Dingle Community Primary School, Kingswinford

BRADLEY

B   radley
R   uns away from his mum and dad
A   nd hates sprouts
D   islikes his bossy, old sister
L   oves to play on his PlayStation
E   ats McDonald's all the time
Y   ucky just like a monster.

Chloe Ghent (7)
Dingle Community Primary School, Kingswinford

JAMES

J   ames
A   jolly boy he is
M   akes people laugh
E   njoys playing funny games
S   kinny he is and has short blondy hair.

Amy Potter (7)
Dingle Community Primary School, Kingswinford

THE WIND

The wind is very strong
He can pick anything up.
He can make leaves dance around your feet.
His hair looks like candyfloss.
His eyes are like thunder.
He has a mouth that's filled with tornadoes.
He has a nose like a car,
His speed gets faster and faster like a rocket.

Jenna Smith (10)
Dingle Community Primary School, Kingswinford

EDWARD

E   dward
D   oesn't like eating meat
W   on't watch Harry Potter
A   nd doesn't like getting dressed
R   iddles are good
D   irties things up sometimes.

Alice Maycock (7)
Dingle Community Primary School, Kingswinford

JAMES

J   ames
A   cts funny just like a bunny
M   akes cakes and
E   ats them all
S   piky hair he has got.

Hannah Williams (7)
Dingle Community Primary School, Kingswinford

FOOTBALL

F ootball is fantastic
O ut on the field time to play
O ptions to score
T ime to really work hard
B all in the top corner
A lbion have scored
L ovely skill by the players
L oyal fans support all the way.

Tom Southall (10)
Dingle Community Primary School, Kingswinford

WEATHER POEM

The lightning smashing around my house
Is like crashing and bashing cymbals
Ruining my house.

The rain showering around my house
Is like a power shower chucking it down.
Pitter-patter-pitter.
With all the weeds squeezing through.

The fog thickening around my house
Is grey, dark and horrible.
Floating and drifting over my grass.

The sunshine is angry around my house
Is a fireball with raging power.
Gravity pulling it down to ground.

Ciara Dullaghan (9)
English Martyrs RC Primary School, Oakham

WEATHER POEM

The rain tapping around my house
Is a tap running in a room
Flowing and pattering
Hitting the walls.

The sunshine burning around my house
Is a bull all worked up
Angry and furious
Bashing the roof.

The thunder rumbling around my house
Is a tiger trying to get in
Crashing and bashing
Clawing on the windows.

Amy Longhurst (9)
English Martyrs RC Primary School, Oakham

RAIN AND SNOW

Rain
The rain tapping around the house
Is tears falling from the sky
Tip tap, tip tap and *splish splosh, splish splosh*
By someone who just cried.

Snow
The snow pattering around the house
Is sugar scattering in the sky
Pit pat, pit pat and settling on the ground
The soft snow drifting onto the roof.

Callum Quigley (9)
English Martyrs RC Primary School, Oakham

WEATHER

The snow swirling around my house,
Is a woollen cloud, soft and spongy,
Beating and battering,
Ruining the daffodils.

The storm, racing around my house,
A battering ram, pummelling the windows,
Fast and furious,
Grappling with the roof.

The hail, whirling around my house,
Bouncing off the windows,
Clattering and pattering,
Grazing the fresh door paint.

Rosie Besant (9)
English Martyrs RC Primary School, Oakham

RAIN AND THUNDER

Rain
The rain pattering around my house
Is a waterfall plunging towards me
Pittering and pattering
At my door.

Thunder
The thunder banging around my house
Is a thief battering on the walls
Bashing and clashing
Sneaking in my door.

Charlie Robertson (10)
English Martyrs RC Primary School, Oakham

THE WEATHER POEM

The lightning, striking around my house
Is the electricity switching on and off.
Crashing and banging
Destroying the roof.

The sun blazing around my house
Is a huge ball of fire.
Hot and burning
Melting the walls.

The rain pattering around my house
Is a power shower being turned on.
Splishing and splashing
Running down my wall.

The fog hovering around my house
Is the fumes out of an exhaust.
Drifting and gliding
Through the letter box on my door.

Thomas Caldicott (11)
English Martyrs RC Primary School, Oakham

WEATHER POEMS

The rain falling around my house
Is a stream rushing and gushing
Tapping and flapping
Falling on the roof.

The thunder banging and crashing around my house.
Like cymbals, like a tiger trying to get in
Banging and
Scratching the windows.

Laura Miller (10)
English Martyrs RC Primary School, Oakham

WEATHER POEM

The rain, pattering around my house
Is God crying in the clouds
Falling and flooding,
Striking at the door.

The fog misting up my house
Is like a ghost, silent in the night
Swirling and filling all space
Drifting on the roof.

The ice setting on the window
Is a sheet of cold glass
Cracking and breaking
Freezing up the roof.

Joseph Nerini (10)
English Martyrs RC Primary School, Oakham

WEATHER

Thunder
The thunder rumbling around my house
Is a giant running at me
Shouting and glaring
Shaking and kicking the house.

Fog
The fog is swirling around our house
Is steam from a kettle
Steamy and smoky
Drifting in my chimney.

Eleanor Mitchell (10)
English Martyrs RC Primary School, Oakham

THE STORM

The storm, howling around my house
Is dark clouds, swarming to and fro,
Clashing and bashing
Damaging the roof.

Wind is knocking around my house
Is stones smashing the house
Banging and clanging
Smashing the windows.

The rain is hitting around my house
Is gloomy clouds, dark
Pitter and patter
Draining the roof.

Oliver Phipps (11)
English Martyrs RC Primary School, Oakham

WEATHER

The lightning
The lightning, flashing around my house
Is Zeus angry and revengeful
Banging and crashing
Flashing at my window.

The rain
The rain, tapping around my house
Is a shower, turned on from Heaven
Splishing and splashing
Whooshing down the roof.

Joe Longhurst (9)
English Martyrs RC Primary School, Oakham

WEATHER POEM

The lightning striking around my house
Is a light switched on and off
Crashing and banging
Destroying the roof.

The thunder crashing around my house
Is the TV turned up too loud
Banging and booming
Deafening the kids.

The storm raging around my house
Is a tornado destroying everything
Gale after gale
Blowing the roof off.

The rain flooding around my house
Is a waterfall cascading over a cliff
Dripping and dropping
Soaking my walls.

Ryan Quinn (11)
English Martyrs RC Primary School, Oakham

WEATHER POEM

The snow covering my house
Is cotton wool falling from the sky
Swirling like a tornado
Drift around the chimney pot.

Hail hitting my house
Is ice balls hitting like bullets
Falling and crashing
Cracking the windows.

Tom Stafford (11)
English Martyrs RC Primary School, Oakham

WEATHER POEM

The rain slashing around my house
Is the fast current of the Indian Ocean
Pittering and pattering
Running down the window.

The snow is crunchy around my house
Is a white, soft, comfortable blanket
Swirling and settling,
Covering the roof.

The sunshine thawing around my house
Is like a radiator and water boiling in a kettle
Scalding and boiling
Toasting the walls.

Jonathan Forster (10)
English Martyrs RC Primary School, Oakham

OUR WORLD

Our planet in the universe is third from the sun,
Green, blue and white blotches, it looks pretty fun.
If you see it from space it looks like a marble,
If you see it through a telescope it looks pretty full.
Different countries, different styles,
Many places, many miles.
Bigger countries, smaller towns,
Lots of people going round.

Zoe Wood (10)
George Betts Primary School, Smethwick

BOYS AND GIRLS

Boys are horrible like noses that are snotty
Boys are very nasty because they pick their botty
They eat nasty things like ketchup on toast
I hate boys because they boast the most.
There are two sides in the house
My dad and brother
And me and my mother.
Also I dislike boys because every second they're playing
with their toys.

Boys and girls never get along
Also in assembly they never sing a song.

Girls are little sweet things, always getting money
And everyone always calls them 'honey'.
They always eat salad
No pizza or bread
They're always tidying their room or fixing the bed.
Girls always eat greens
Never eat beans
They watch TV
Scream when they see a bee
They don't like dogs
And don't play in bogs.

Rheanne Bailey (11)
George Betts Primary School, Smethwick

SAM'S RAP

I want to go to a party
I want to go to school
I want to go to shops
Or shoot some pool.

I like to play with my friends
I like to watch TV
But at the weekends
I just want to be me.

When it's time for dinner
I eat all of my food
Oops, sorry I burped
I didn't mean to be rude.

If I'm not playing
Or watching the toons
I'm just chilling out
Listening to my tunes.

Sam Lundy (10)
George Betts Primary School, Smethwick

DANCING

I love my dancing
to show off my moves
other people do the same
but have different grooves.

People buy fancy dresses
to make them look pretty
all the adults say, 'Ah bless, ain't that pretty.'
But I think some are niffy.

My friends also do dancing
they're really, really good.
They have been to loads of competitions
and have just won and won and won.

If we win a competition
we have to go to Blackpool
and dance the weekend away
but the judges walk round
the dance floor looking like a fool!

Kirsty Louise Macdonald (10)
George Betts Primary School, Smethwick

CRICKET

Sandeep is my name
And cricket is my game
DT is my favourite subject
Science too.

Writing is enjoyable
Especially writing a
Poem for you.

Over and underarm
Bowling, running as fast
As I can, going to catch
The ball in my hands.

Usually save the ball,
Might I catch it, might I not.
A little bit further to the right,
Now I've got it, hip hip hooray!

Sandeep Ghuman (10)
George Betts Primary School, Smethwick

MY ADVENTURE TO INDIA

As I walk through the villages
Smelling fresh food
Playing with my dude
Having hot fresh dhal with rice
With mango chutney
Looking at the golden temple
Having a sunbathe in the hot and shimmering sun
While eating my bun
Praying to God
Hoping I see my family
Again I walk through the villages
Buying some gifts
Again I eat some spicy, hot cashew nuts
Drinking a cold mango juice
Sweating with the sun
All the noises, the lorries and people
Walking and driving along the dusty and smelly road
Bags of rubbish all dumped on the road
All the smells going up my nose
But I visit the Ganges
See my face in the water while a tear falls down
I have seen all my life here in India
But I have to say goodbye to my fellow friends.

Jaspreet Kaur (10)
George Betts Primary School, Smethwick

FRIENDS FOREVER

I have a very best friend
A really trustworthy friend,
We laugh at the same things
And like the same rings.

She likes rabbits
And I like cats
We aren't keen on bats
And have no mats.

I have a really trustworthy friend
We share all our secrets,
And at the end of school
We are always laughing.

She is the only friend
Who's the best in the world,
I couldn't find another
Just like her.

We have lots of fun
At each other's houses,
Also at school
When we are feeling down.

When she's around
Nobody's glum,
She turns our world
The right way up.

My true friend.

Louise Harris (11)
George Betts Primary School, Smethwick

MY SPECIAL DREAM

I have a dream
Going to America
To meet the stars
As I eat my Mars
As the flag shines
Through my eyes
As I walk to the Statue of Liberty
Praying to God I see it
Birds flying high in the skies
As people eat their pies
As I see my whole life in America
Walking along all the streets
As they get busier
I think about what I should do
Praying to God I see the zoo
I see all the Disney characters
Doing a parade
In the streets of *America*
Winnie the Pooh and Piglet too
All the others helping too
Help me find something to do
Thinking about my family
What they're up to
I finally realise it was just a dream
Why couldn't it be true?
I keep thinking about my dream
It just wants me to scream
Help me mom what should I do?

Anisha Kumari (10)
George Betts Primary School, Smethwick

INDIA

As I am walking through
the village,
smelling fresh mango
being cut,
I see coconuts being
smashed open.
Now I am walking
back to my bungalow
taking in some deep
fresh air,
I pass the Golden Temple
and its gold shines.
It's just amazing.
I sit beside its water to
pray to God.
I see the whole of Bollywood
The famous stars
acting and shooting their films.
My bungalow is now here.
I can see my mum
cooking curry and chapattis.
My journey is finished.
Now I've explored
the whole of India,
I wonder what place is
next . . .

Jasdeep Matharu (11)
George Betts Primary School, Smethwick

My Journey To India

Tasting red, yummy fish with cow's milk,
Tasting sweet fruit from the trees
Tasting white chapattis with dhal too.

Seeing big lovely sights,
Seeing different kinds of animals
Seeing my grandparents.

Hearing the animals making noises at night,
Hearing people shout and yell
Hearing scooters go by.

Smelling lots of rubbish on the road,
Smelling tasty food from far away
Smelling my mum's perfume.

Touching cats, dogs, rabbits and horses
Touching people left to right
Touching the nice blue sea.

Raveena Gill (11)
George Betts Primary School, Smethwick

Pizza

I like to eat lots of pizza
But I thought they had lots of pips
But when pizza touches my lips
The pizza turns into ships.

I like lots of pizza
So when I bite the pizza I start to fizz
But when I drink some Coke
I always whiz.

Jake Haston (8)
Glenmere CP School, Wigston

WHAT IS IN MY SHOPPING BASKET?

Come into the supermarket then you all shall see
what is in my shopping basket to take home with me.
Lots of pasta
make me faster
Lots of pizza
for my teacher
Lots of cheese
to make me sneeze
And lots of candy
makes me dandy.
One day I went to Asda to see what food they had
and some of it was good, and some of it was bad.
Yucky toffee
tastes like coffee.
Horrid cake
tastes like steak.
Yucky jam
tastes like ham,
and horrid honey
makes me go funny.
Now you see what I like and what I don't for my tea.
So if you want something to eat,
well come along with me.

Freya Vincent (8)
Glenmere CP School, Wigston

YUCKY YUCK YUCK!

Round, small, oval slugs go nice with girls called Hetti,
But I prefer jellyfish nails with my green tagliatelli.
Limey, muddy, brown apples with maggots crawling fast,
If I consume this apple, I don't know how long I'm going to last.

I jumped out into the garden and quickly got stung by a bee,
I shouted, 'Hip, hip hooray, yihee, yihee, yihee.'

Why on earth did I just say that if I just got stung by a bee?
Is it the food I ate or did I eat a pea?
Could the pea be something from my brain
Or was it from my friend called Kathryn Wayne?

Oh!
Please someone tell me
For goodness sake I've got a bee sting on my face,
Now I can't go in and eat my pizza base,
My mum is inside!
Help!

Hafsah Ali (8)
Glenmere CP School, Wigston

STRAWBERRIES

Strawberries are nice to munch.
They're far better than yucky pears.
Because they're easy to crunch.
They never give you the fears.

Strawberries are not round like a ball
They're like some shape that's like a pie.
It's not like you crash and fall
It's some shape that's like an eye.

Stefan Bullous (8)
Glenmere CP School, Wigston

CHOCOLATE BISCUITS

Chocolate biscuits are yummy,
Don't eat too many of these
Or you'll get an upset tummy.
Chocolate biscuits are gooey and chewy
And they are really nice.
Chocolate biscuits may be yummy
But are very bad for you.
If you're very greedy
The best thing to do is hide from everybody else.

Josh Kirk (8)
Glenmere CP School, Wigston

ICE CREAM

I wonder what ice cream is made of?
Is it made of mould because it's so cold.
Or is it made of mice because it's so nice.
Or maybe it is made of cream?
Oh, what a dream!

Rose Ashton (8)
Glenmere CP School, Wigston

CHOCOLATE BISCUITS

Chocolate biscuits are my favourite
I could eat them every day.
They are very, very chocolatey
In a very delicious way.

Jordan Wills (8)
Glenmere CP School, Wigston

CAKES

I like cakes, I like cakes.

Bake them in the oven.
I like cakes
Eat them when they're baked.

I like cakes, I like cakes,
Put them in the oven.
I like cakes, I like cakes,
Eat them with your flake.

I like cakes, I like cakes
Bake them if you want.
I like cakes, I like cakes
Eat them in the day.

I like cakes, I like cakes,
Eat them when they're ready
I like cakes, I like cakes
Chuck them in the bin if you don't like them!

Jamie Wright (8)
Glenmere CP School, Wigston

FUDGE

Fudge is golden and sweet.
When you put it in your mouth it sticks when you eat.
If you take it out and it is all chewed up
It will look like a piece of chewed up meat.
I would keep it in if I were you
Before your mum comes in
So keep eating
But if you do take it out.
Keep it a secret.

Arthur Redfern (9)
Glenmere CP School, Wigston

CHIPS

Chips, chips are the best
They're not like the other rest.
They look a lovely yellowy-cream,
Just like a wonderful dream.
Chips, chips are the best
Not like pizza, yuck!
I wish the world only had chips . . . but . . . no luck.
I couldn't eat tomatoes, no, no, no, no, no
I hate tomatoes
But I like chips though.
Chips, chips are the best
I'll never like the other rest.

Jessica Cooper (8)
Glenmere CP School, Wigston

BUGS

Slugs and snails are my favourite
Bees on sandwiches I hate.
Flies and worms on toast I like
Ants and bugs stay in their tunnels
Waiting for bait.

While the bugs and ants are looking for bait
Slugs and snails are snoozing
And the worms and flies have been eaten
And they go flying into Heaven.

William Haston (8)
Glenmere CP School, Wigston

WHAT MY UNCLE LIKES TO EAT

What my uncle likes to eat
Are some very yucky treats
Like toenails and bat breath with just a bit of blood.
What about ladybird cake with a sprinkle of mud.

He will also scoff fish eggs and earwax meat
Then for pudding a sheep that will still bleat.
There the foods he will munch,
But he'll never sip fruit punch.

He is like a wolf, lion, ant and platypus
He'd even eat these on a 99 bus.
Jonathan Bloggs eats all the same things
But! He eats other very big wings.

Nisha Gorania (8)
Glenmere CP School, Wigston

GRAPES

Grapes are sweet and juicy
I gave one to my best friend Lucy.
She said they're yummy
Because we could hear them in our tummies.

Grapes are sweet.
They are the best to eat.
Don't gobble or stop
Because you'll wobble and then . . .
Pop!

Katie Deacon (9)
Glenmere CP School, Wigston

SWEETS AND CAKES

Sweets, sweets, wonderful sweets.
Some are round,
Some are square,
Some are even neat.

Cakes, cakes, wonderful cakes.
Some are round,
Some are square,
Some are even neat.

Freddie Dobrijevic (9)
Glenmere CP School, Wigston

DONUTS

Chocolate donuts fresh from the bake
But if you don't like donuts
Why don't you have a cake?
Donuts with custard and cream
And they are such a dream.
Donuts with sugar and sprinkles
Gives me the tinkles.

Frankie Sharman (9)
Glenmere CP School, Wigston

WORMS

Long, thin, juicy worms go nicely with spaghetti.
But lemony slugs and sausages with mud go better with tagliatelli.
Of course I forgot buttered fly, a scrumptious dish for me
But what I really, really like is rabbit's ears for tea.

Kathryn Reynolds (9)
Glenmere CP School, Wigston

WHAT DAD LOVES TO EAT

My dad is a very unhealthy man.
He does not fry anything in the pan!
He is a silly Dad
People think he is so mad.

He scoffs spiders, worms, rabbit food, bird seed.
Ear wax and ants.
When he ate his dinner he shouted, 'Oh thanks.'
That's what my dad eats.

Amy Brown (8)
Glenmere CP School, Wigston

GRAPES

There once was a grape in the garden.
It was like blue ink from a pen
It shined bright in the light
The wind in the air bounced the grape in the sky.
Then I said, 'Oh well, I'll wait 'til next year.'

Oliver Stone (8)
Glenmere CP School, Wigston

JELLY

Orange jelly, red jelly, yellow jelly, all wobbling on the plate,
Wibble-wobble, wibble-wobble, munch, munch, munch.
Orange jelly, red jelly, yellow jelly in my belly.

Make some more orange jelly, red jelly, yellow jelly, *splat,*
No more orange jelly, red jelly, yellow jelly for me.

Aimee Harris (9)
Glenmere CP School, Wigston

BUGS

Bugs are horrible,
My sister says they're nice,
I say not as good as rice.
My sister likes the black ones.
I don't like any ones.

Sometimes I have to eat them at school
Before we go to the swimming pool.
My sister doesn't have to
But she wishes she could do.

Jodie Langley (9)
Glenmere CP School, Wigston

TIGERS

Tigers have stripes
Orange and black
Stripes on their tummies
And stripes on their backs!

Tigers have teeth
Which are called jaws
Tigers have paws
And on them sharp claws!

Tigers are like lions
Not in golds or yellows
But they're big and strong
They're lovely fellows!

Tigers are good at hiding
In grass with sunlight
So be very careful
Or he'll give you a bite!

Hannah Stevens (9)
Hurst Green Primary School, Halesowen

WHAT AM I?

Spotty like a cheetah,
Colourful like a rainbow,
What am I?

Cute like a kitten,
Silent like a lioness,
What am I?

Small like a wriggly worm,
Quick like a jaguar,
What am I?

I am the ceiling walker,
I am a small lizard,
I am a *gecko!*

Katie Danks *(8)*
Hurst Green Primary School, Halesowen

THE WEIRD CHAIR

When my teacher talked,
My chair always walked,
And when walked,
It also talked.

But after that my chair went,
Because it had a big dent,
That was the end of the chair,
So I'll leave my story there.

Antonia Veal *(9)*
Hurst Green Primary School, Halesowen

THE LION

The lion is a mighty tree
standing firm and proud,
silent like a jaguar thumping
on the ground!

The lion is yellow, yellow like the sun,
if you ever see it,
you'd better start to *run!*

The lion has a beautiful mane,
going down his back,
it's full of gaudy colours
no part of it is black!

The lion is so strong
it could kill you with one blow,
that would hurt you *ow, ow, ow!*

Oliver Rogers (8)
Hurst Green Primary School, Halesowen

RABBIT POEM

R   unning through the fields is so much fun
A   s cuddly as a soft toy
B   eautiful white fur as white as the snow
B   rown soft paws
I   live in a hole
T   errific animal indeed.

Tyler Shutts (8)
Hurst Green Primary School, Halesowen

DOLPHINS

Dolphins are smooth
Dolphins are slim
They can jump up high
And they have five fins
Their fins are like a car tyre.

The dolphins have two little eyes
I think they are nice.
They can go deep underwater without
taking a breath.

They are really, really rubbery
And super strong and fast,
So if you go on holiday
Look out, look out for the
                    Dolphin.

David Alsop (8)
Hurst Green Primary School, Halesowen

DOLPHIN POEM

I am a dolphin loud and strong
My shiny back glittery all day long.
I make a funny squeaky noise,
I jump around the sea,
And as well as all the animals
I play with the seaweed
Which are my toys.

Laura Hayfield (9)
Hurst Green Primary School, Halesowen

SCHOOL PHOTO ALBUM

That's me
Struggling hard with sticks
Falling about
Pity it's not made of bricks.

That's me
Messing about with elastic bands
They kept snapping
And flying from my hands.

That's me
Fixing my sticks
Doing my joints
Making sure I don't get in a mix.

That's me
Checking the joints
Looking closely
Making sure there aren't any sharp points.

Benjamin Timmington-Taylor (9)
Hurst Green Primary School, Halesowen

LIONS

Lions have cubs,
Lions look like tigers
And leopards,
Lions are funny,
As funny as can be,
Lions are big
Very, very big.

Ben Kirton (9)
Hurst Green Primary School, Halesowen

PARROT

Eats lots of seeds
For all its feeds.

Claws like a made
Carved spade.

Mouth like metal
Stings like a nettle.

It's very soft
It lives in a loft.

Fast like a Jaguar
But don't let it drag you.

Bites like a metal
Strong like a nettle.

Laughs like a kettle
Sounds like it's metal.

Naughty but does daring deeds
After he is in need.

Joshua Collett (9)
Hurst Green Primary School, Halesowen

THE SHARK

I swim with a grin up to greet you
See how my jaws open wide
Why don't you come a bit closer?
Please, take a good look inside.

Arran Dhillon (8)
Hurst Green Primary School, Halesowen

COMODO DRAGON

C omodo dragons are as big as wagons
O h no one has bitten me
M y house is a lizard farm
O ut my nest.
D amn I am picked to get lizard eggs
O ranges are my favourite fruit.

D eer is my favourite dinner
R oaming through the jungle
A dders can kill me with one bite
G reen leaves surround me in my land
O verlooking African plains
N othing else to say except dinner.

Joseph Rose (9)
Hurst Green Primary School, Halesowen

THE POLAR BEAR

The polar bear is cuddly and cute,
He lives in a cave.
He has lots of thick white fur
And is very big and brave.

He eats lots of fish and seals,
That will make him get fat.
He has got big legs and nasty paws,
That makes him have a chat.

Tom Blears (8)
Hurst Green Primary School, Halesowen

JAGUAR

Fast as a leopard,
Runs like a jeep,
Always fierce,
Never asleep!

Cute as a cuddly toy,
Rare as a tiger,
Fierce as a bear
And has a lot of hair!

It's very, very rare,
Isn't bare,
Doesn't fight fair
And has a lair!

Bradley Clarke (8)
Hurst Green Primary School, Halesowen

THE JAGUAR

Cute as a cuddly toy
Fast as lightning
Dangerous as fire
Rare as a polar bear
He kills animals for his prey
Colourful as a rainbow
As fierce as the killer shark
As cute as a pussy cat
Puffed up like a car
Endangered as a tiger
Teeth as sharp as razors
Soft paws and very sharp claws.

James Wythes (8)
Hurst Green Primary School, Halesowen

BUZZARD

Buzzard circles high
In the sky,
Looking for its prey
So what does it say?

He is as brown as mud
Watch the meat from where he stood.
His wings will take you on a cloud
When he shoots he is very loud.

Isaac Kelly (8)
Hurst Green Primary School, Halesowen

THE SPIDER

A spider is creeping along the floor
so fast soon it will be up the wall.
A spider is hairy and black, it's got hairs
all over its back.
A spider has eight legs,
all of them as long as pegs.
A spider has eight eyes and with them he catches flies.

Christian Goodgame (8)
Hurst Green Primary School, Halesowen

TOAD

Is as fast as a ball
Slow as a turtle
As brown as a tree
As fat as it can be.

James Hanson (8)
Hurst Green Primary School, Halesowen

MY FAMILY SIMILES

My grandad's Dad has a beard
like Santa Claus'.

My grandad smiles and laughs
like a professional clown.

My grandma smiles and her nose
wrinkles and is big as Pinocchio's nose.

My uncle's hands are as thin
as a stick.

My brother has yellow teeth
like a ravishing sun.

My brother speaks like an alien to me.

And best of all they all love me.
          I hope.

Kyra Rai (9)
Hurst Green Primary School, Halesowen

SHARK

I swim with a grin up to greet you
See how my jaws open wide
Why don't you come a bit closer?
Please take a good look inside.

See my sharp burning teeth
Why don't you come a bit closer?
Please take a good look inside.

Yes I'm a shark, come, come a bit closer,
And I will gobble you alive.

Andrew Irving (9)
Hurst Green Primary School, Halesowen

SNAKE

I am an anaconda
I am slimy and rough
My body is as long as forty metres
I slither all day and night
My eyes are beady and dark red
If you touch me I will bite you in half.
         Ssss! Yum-yum!

Daniel Marsh (8)
Hurst Green Primary School, Halesowen

CAT

I am proud
My body is as ginger as a goldfish
And my voice is very soft
When I talk it comes out in a marvellous miaow
My eyes are as colourful as the sunset
I live in a warm, cosy basket,
My tail sways across your face as you stroke my fluffy back.

Rebekah Swain (9)
Hurst Green Primary School, Halesowen

FLAMINGO

I am beautiful.
I am as pink as a strawberry ice cream.
My legs are as long as the Twin Towers.
When I eat, the bones on the fish crunch
like chains are rattling
and I stand on one leg sometimes.

Leah Eckesley (8)
Hurst Green Primary School, Halesowen

THE LION

I am a lion who hunts for my prey
I am fast and eat delicious food
I am the king of all lions
I can snatch people
I love to eat people
My head is so hairy
My eyes are as blue as the sea
My tail swishes up and down
My back is as fur
My belly is as bouncy as jelly
My body is like a lion
    Drip! Drip!
    Drip! Drip!

Alex Byatt (8)
Hurst Green Primary School, Halesowen

MY GRANDAD

My grandad's teeth are yellow like sour juicy lemons
He is like an athlete, whenever we go canoeing
He always comes first,
He runs quite fast, he's like a cheetah.
My grandad's head is shaped like an oval upside down.
He's got a nose long like a pointy carrot.
When my grandad looks at me he smiles and does it happily.
Best of all he's my grandad and he's the best you could ever wish for.

Amy Davies (8)
Hurst Green Primary School, Halesowen

MY GRANDPA

My grandpa is tall and as golden as the Eiffel Tower.
My grandpa is as strong as a rhino.
My grandpa is as smart as Gareth Gates.
My grandpa has wriggly, crunchy veins
like a McDonald's bag of chips.
My grandpa thinks like the world's brainiest kids.
My grandpa walks like a beautiful peacock
that is proud of its tail.
Best of all my grandpa stares like a zombie
at the news on the television.
        That's him!

Jagpreet Ghuman (9)
Hurst Green Primary School, Halesowen

LION

I am king of the important jungle,
My teeth are shiny as the sun.
My eyes wander viciously.
My fur is orange, as burning fire.
When people look at my face they are very scared.

My claws are sharp as a shark's tooth.
When my enemies come near I roar with power.
My greatest enemy is the black panther.
When the enemy is near, I growl to warn others.
                Rrrr!

Jamie Gill (9)
Hurst Green Primary School, Halesowen

LION

I am the king
King of the jungle
I am as hairy as a gorilla
My eyes are as fierce as can be
When I walk everyone screams
When I talk I just say *roar!*
At night
When it is black as a blackboard
I take a swim in the deep gigantic pool
But best of all I am the king of the jungle.

Rooooaarr!

Jordan Gibbs *(8)*
Hurst Green Primary School, Halesowen

MY GRANDPA

My grandpa is as bendy as a caterpillar
As tough as a fierce crocodile
My grandpa is older than an ancient mummy
As soft as good old Scooby-Doo
He laughs like a little bird
He's as big as a massive elephant
My grandpa sits like the Prime Minister
And I sit on his lap
But best of all I love my grandpa
And he loves me.

Ben Churchill *(8)*
Hurst Green Primary School, Halesowen

BLACK PANTHER

I am a black panther
I am faster than a tiger
I'm darker than the midnight sky
With eyes that flash in misty moon
And teeth sharper than a knife
With sharp eyes.
I am as big as a flat
I can run faster than a bullet.
Time to catch my prey.
Snap
Snap
Yum
Yum
Goodnight
Zzzzzzzzz.

Alex Cox (9)
Hurst Green Primary School, Halesowen

MY FRIEND

My friend's hair is as brown as a cat
Her face is as pale as sand
Her body is as cuddly as a bear
Her lips are as red as lipstick
She is as straight as a white lamp post
She dresses like the Queen
She is as cool as a snowman
The best thing about Leah is,
She is a good friend.

Megan Evans (9)
Hurst Green Primary School, Halesowen

HAMSTER

I am special!
I eat and I sleep.
I scratch and I nibble.
I bite and I *annoy* people.
For when I go on my wheel.
When I drink loudly from my bottle
And for when I bite your fingers *off.*
It's not my fault you torment me
When you know I'm only small and delicate.

I am very lonely!
I live in a stubby cage on my own.
I would love to get out of my cage,
And be free like the wind.
But I hate it when my owners find out
And shout in my tiny little ears.
                Save me!

Sara Lee (9)
Hurst Green Primary School, Halesowen

LION

I am king of the jungle!
You will never hear me cry
My tummy will never stop and grumble
I am king because I can't tell a lie, or can I?
Every time I say hello, everyone is scared.

  Roar!

Adam Scott (8)
Hurst Green Primary School, Halesowen

I'M A MONKEY

I am the cheekiest out of all the animals in the zoo.
I am brown as a tree.
My eyes are like two glazed, cheeky eyes shining happily.
When I walk I'm like a kid.
I sit all day eating delicious bananas,
And it fills my tum, yum-yum,
And I go on adventures climbing from tree to tree.
When I laugh I sound cheeky
And I drink lovely blue water.
        Uahahahaha!

Rebecca Hanley (8)
Hurst Green Primary School, Halesowen

TIGER

I am the king of the jungle
My red and yellow stripes are bright as a fire
My eyes are as dark as the midnight sky
When I walk I stamp for my prey
I growl louder than a factory
When I laugh I go ha, ha, ha
My job is to frighten the other animals
Because they won't let me go to sleep.
When I see people I go yum-yum!

        Roar!

Ryan Wainwright (9)
Hurst Green Primary School, Halesowen

The Dog

I am a dog, very sensitive indeed.
My owner tells me to be quiet
but it only makes me bark louder.
When guests come, I jump up them and bark to get attention.
People say I am like a sheep
I am as white as snow
But I am definitely not slow.
I can run very fast especially
through the mud.
Then I like to watch my owners mop the floor.
Woof, woof!

Holly McKnight (9)
Hurst Green Primary School, Halesowen

The Lion

I am the king
I am as furry as a carpet
My eyes are like the blue of the sea
When I walk I am like a posh person
My teeth shine in the sun
I like to eat meat
You'd better be alert
The lion's coming to eat you.
Snap, yum
Snap, yum.

Joseph Upton (8)
Hurst Green Primary School, Halesowen

SABRE-TOOTHED TIGER

I am strong,
I am as yellow as a banana.
My eyes are like the midnight moon.
When I growl I'm like a growling bear.
My fangs are as sharp as a knife.
I am as big as a lion,
But as small as an elephant.
I am as tough as a mammoth.
I am as cuddly as a toy bear.
I am as scary as a tiger,
And when I creep up to my prey!
Snap!
Snap!
Yum!
Yum
And claws like a black panther
With teeth like one too.
When I roar, I roar like a cheetah.

Roar!

Jamie O'Toole (9)
Hurst Green Primary School, Halesowen

MY GRANDPA

My grandpa is as gentle as a tiny teddy
His eyes sparkle like a shining star
His hair stands on end like green grass
His face is as fresh as a rabbit
When he walks he limps like a frog
When he sleeps he snores like a gigantic giant
But best of all he is the best grandpa in the world.

Conor Devaney (8)
Hurst Green Primary School, Halesowen

LION

I am king
But I cannot sing
When I walk
People talk
I live in the jungle
Where all the trees are a jumble
When my enemy is near
I roar to cause fear
When I roar
Your ears will be sore
Who am I?
Guess who I am?

    A lion
       Rraaahh.

Grant Meredith (9)
Hurst Green Primary School, Halesowen

CAT

I am as black as oil
I am as brown as mud
My eyes are as dark as the midnight sky
My tail is as flappy as a fan
I am as fat as a building
My head is as round as a football
My claws are as sharp as a dagger
My legs are as long as a ruler
You wouldn't want to catch me in a dark alley.

    Miaow!

Lewis Carey (9)
Hurst Green Primary School, Halesowen

SNAP GOES CROCODILE

I am a crocodile
I live in the wild.
All the time I am so vicious
I am as green as grass in people's backyards.
My feet are smaller than yours, because they're
Even smaller than a pen top.
But you wouldn't believe how sharp my teeth are
Because they're sharper than a razor blade.
My stomach is as thin as a leg off a chair.
But the last part of my body is my tail
And my tail is stronger than super glue.

My wish for the future
Is to have some
Yummy snacks
Yum-yum!

James Burton (8)
Hurst Green Primary School, Halesowen

LOVE

Love is the colour orange,
It smells like daffodils,
It tastes like strawberries,
It sounds like children laughing,
It feels like fluffy soft feathers,
Love lives in the garden of happiness.

Becky Hale (10)
Hurst Green Primary School, Halesowen

IN A BUS

I'm in a bus,
I can hear the driver whistling,
Babies are crying,
Children singing.
I can see cars zooming past,
I can also see gigantic buildings.
I can smell the diesel,
Cars are growling at each other.
The ice-cold air is coming through the window,
Angry horns making a noise.
It's raining cats and dogs,
Merryhill is in sight
Closer, closer, closer,
We're there!

Liam Gray (9)
Hurst Green Primary School, Halesowen

MY GRANDMA

My gran is as small as a tin
Her hair is like a curly ring of smoke
Her eyes are like sparkling blue diamonds
Her face is as smooth and soft as a feather
When she walks she is as slow as a turtle
When she sits she is like a cute teddy bear
When she laughs she is like a laughing hyena
When she sleeps she is like a sleeping quiet fish
The best thing about my gran is when she gives me ten sausage rolls.
I like my gran, she always tickles me.

Chloe Edwards (8)
Hurst Green Primary School, Halesowen

ANGER

Anger is black as coal,
Anger smells like hot ashes,
Anger feels like a sharp pain,
Anger looks like a volcano erupting,
Anger tastes like bitter lemon.

Stephen Scott (10)
Hurst Green Primary School, Halesowen

UP IN THE ATTIC

Photos piled on special events
Christmas trees so new and bright
And toys so old they are falling apart.
Baby clothes so old and messy.
Spiders scuttling over brown old boxes.
Up in the attic, cold and damp.

Laura Mayes (10)
Hurst Green Primary School, Halesowen

SADNESS

Sadness is a gloomy black,
It smells like a newly lit match,
It tastes like bad milk,
It feels painful,
It lives in the dark forest.

Cory Laidlaw (10)
Hurst Green Primary School, Halesowen

LIVING WITH BROTHERS!

Brothers are a pain
They have a strange brain
They twist you round the bend
Mostly up the wall
They bounce a football all the time
They like to sing a song
Always rock stars
Sometimes I think they're on planet Mars
I hate living with brothers!

Sophie Byatt (10)
Hurst Green Primary School, Halesowen

JOY

Joy is blue
It smells like pie
It tastes like your favourite food
It sounds like birds singing in a tree
Joy lives in the middle of your heart.

Jonathan Guy (10)
Hurst Green Primary School, Halesowen

JOY

Joy is blue.
It smells like the flowers of spring.
It tastes like sugar and strawberries.
It feels like a warm, cosy bed
And it lives in our hearts.

Tom Kavanagh (10)
Hurst Green Primary School, Halesowen

NIGHTMARES

When Mom comes up,
And says, 'Go to sleep,'
That's when I close my eyes,
Then the nightmare makers take a peep.

Dreams of monsters,
Dreams of ghosts,
Dreams of things,
You hate the most.

Georgina Rowe (10)
Hurst Green Primary School, Halesowen

HOPE

Hope is yellow,
It smells like a sweet honey scent,
It feels warm and cosy,
It tastes like vanilla ice cream,
Hope lives in the heart of the sun.

Mandeep Johal (10)
Hurst Green Primary School, Halesowen

ANGER

Anger is black,
It smells like fire,
Anger feels like something stabbing you,
It tastes mouldy,
It sounds like a balloon bursting,
Anger lives in a volcano.

Kirsty Slater (9)
Hurst Green Primary School, Halesowen

THE BEST PET

My pet has eight legs,
my pet is a meat eater,
my pet is hairy,
my pet can be dangerous,
he also sheds his skin,
he is a pet you can't forget,
he is a spiky
            spider!

Amanda Smith (9)
Hurst Green Primary School, Halesowen

LOVE

Love is pink,
It smells like red roses,
It tastes like delicious chocolate cake,
It sounds like the rustling in the trees,
And it lives in your heart.

Katie Manison (10)
Hurst Green Primary School, Halesowen

HAPPY

Happy is yellow, it smells like popcorn
It tastes like sweets,
It sounds noisy like a volcano.
It feels sharp and hard.
It lives in your heart.

Sunjay Virdee (10)
Hurst Green Primary School, Halesowen

MY LITTLE SISTER

My little sister
is as sweet as a rose.
She really laughs
when I tickle her nose.

My big brother
is as clever as me.
He loves his wrestling
so he does try and break my knee.

My young mother
is really kind.
When we are lost,
she will always look behind.

My beautiful dad
is into fast cars.
He is really strong,
so he can break bars.

Megan Loone (9)
Hurst Green Primary School, Halesowen

BUTTERFLY

A butterfly is pretty as a flower.
It can fly high up to a tower.
Flutters like leaves.
Blowing in a breeze.
Like two big eyes.
Flying to the sunrise.
Blue, yellow, green
Playing as a team.

Meera Nayyar (9)
Hurst Green Primary School, Halesowen

SORRY SIR!

'Late again Ashcroft!'
'Yes Sir,'
'What's the excuse this time?'
'It wasn't my fault Sir,'
'Whose was it then?'
'Grandma's Sir,'
'What's happened?'
'She's dead Sir!'
'Again!'
'Yes Sir,'
'That's four grandmothers this week!'
'I know, it's very sad Sir,'
'And what about the test Ashcroft?'
'It was the dentist Sir,'
'Did he die too?'
'No, Sir, he was in a tornado Sir,'
'Then what?'
'He died Sir,'
'Why didn't you do PE?'
'My kit hasn't been ironed Sir!'
'Why?'
'Forgot to ask . . .'
'Who usually does it?'
'Grandma Sir!'

Jon Ashcroft (9)
Hurst Green Primary School, Halesowen

EMOTIONS OF LIFE

Hope is orange,
It looks bright and shiny
It feels happy and great
Hope lives in our hearts.

Anger is bright red,
It looks nasty and evil
It feels bad and wicked
Anger lives in a volcano.

Happiness is yellow like the sun,
It looks fun and great
It feels like a hug and a cuddle
Happiness lives in everything.

Evil is dull blue,
It looks ugly and dirty
It feels nasty and violent
Evil lives in the badness of our souls.

Old age is grey,
It looks weird and wrinkly
It feels rusty and ancient
Old age lives inside people very old.

Love is rosy-red,
It looks like a newborn child
It feels warm and cosy
Love lives in your heart.

Jennifer Watkins (10)
Hurst Green Primary School, Halesowen

MY BABY COUSIN ABBI

My baby cousin Abbi,
Is a bit flabby.
She looks very cute,
In her Aston Villa suit.

She has a nice mom and dad,
Who loves her when she is sad.
She has a cute face,
Her other cousin is Grace.

She has short hair,
And mine is fair.
She has long nails
She's heavy on the scales.

Emily Barber (10)
Hurst Green Primary School, Halesowen

THE HAUNTED HOUSE

Spooky skeletons tugging at your feet,
Thunder banging out in the street.

Ghouls and ghosts come out to play,
Vampires, monsters, please go away.

Mom will have a fit when I go home,
My hair's sticking up, where's my comb?

Phew! I'm not going there again,
        Are you?

Megan Hunter (9)
Hurst Green Primary School, Halesowen

CAR

My car is burning red
It has a horn, that roars
My car is as fast as a jet,
And the wind is as strong as Superman
And is raining cats and dogs.

James Snelleksz (9)
Hurst Green Primary School, Halesowen

SADNESS

A colour to describe sadness is blue,
Sadness smells like the salt in the sea,
Sadness tastes like butter, dry, salty air
Sadness sounds like the sea's waves
Crashing against the walls.

Thomas Byrne (11)
Hurst Green Primary School, Halesowen

WINDY DAYS . . .

Wind flies and glides about.
Wind pushes me without a doubt.
Wind hustles and bustles.
Wind blows and mows the lawn.
Wind fights about with kites.
Wind gusts and blusters.
Wind climbs up trees.
Then becomes a breeze.

Tom King (9)
Leighfield Primary School, Oakham

THE HOLOCAUST

T ables upturned by Nazi soldiers.
H urried without choice to stuffy ghettos.
E laborate lifestyles are no more.

H ubbub is the packed cattle trucks
O verpowering odour
L abour by day, coldness by night
O nly feeling helplessness and confusion
C herished people getting weaker
A lways seeing families split
U nder clouds of betrayal
S oon we must give up all hope
T error and fear slowly leaving.
    The Americans are here!

Catherine Ludolf (10)
Leighfield Primary School, Oakham

JUST REMEMBER

Just remember,
What you did in the past,
Naughty or good,
Time flies fast.
Just remember
The first person you saw,
Maybe more than I,
Or even more.

Just remember,
The first time you walked,
How good it felt,
Like when you talked.

Ellen Gregory (9)
Leighfield Primary School, Oakham

THAT WAS A SAD DAY

She was purry
She was furry.
She was all that you could wish for
And I gave her fish for her dinner.
That was a happy day when my cat was alive.

She was black, she was white,
She slept with me at night.
I loved her to bits,
And she loved me too.
That was a happy day when my cat was alive.

I felt for her,
She was gone,
What was happening?
It felt wrong.
That was a sad day when my cat died.

I looked out the window,
It was still night.

A screech, a miaow
A flash of lights.
That was a sad day when my cat died.

I thought it was a dream
In the morning I looked.
Sure enough I saw her,
My cat was . . .
That was a sad day when my cat died.

Ruth Corbet (10)
Leighfield Primary School, Oakham

THE RACE

With my heart pounding,
I stood up to start,
Ready, steady, go!
It happened so fast.

The others zoomed off,
I was left behind,
What came next?
It made me start to cry.

Blubbering like a baby,
Everyone was staring,
Tears down my face,
But nobody was caring.

The race went on,
My team won, but I never ran a race again!

Joanna Partridge (9)
Leighfield Primary School, Oakham

THE MOON

It shone brighter than ever,
It twinkled like a star,
It lay upon the sleeping world,
Watching us as we dream,
It lit the dark paths to our dream,
I fear the morning for it will be gone,
Enjoy the night, I shall
For tonight it shall be my last night
With the moon by my side.

Georgia Huzar (9)
Leighfield Primary School, Oakham

OUR CATS

Tigger is our ginger cat.
He purrs a lot and likes to scratch.
But now he's gone away,
And we look for him each day.

Jigsaw is our funny cat
She hates being hugged,
And likes to flap,
And when we turn out the light,
She closes her eyes and purrs goodnight.

Daisy is our calm cat
She never goes away
She sleeps upon my bed at night
And keeps me feeling safe.

Isabella Winkley (8)
Leighfield Primary School, Oakham

FIREWORKS

Shooting stars swirl
Rockets whirl
Bangers bang
It's Bonfire Night
Sparklers dazzle
Fountains blaze
Roman candles flicker
It's Bonfire Night
Firecrackers shower
Catherine wheels hiss
Its ashes left,
It's Bonfire Night.

Hannah McCreesh (9)
Leighfield Primary School, Oakham

AUTUMN DAYS

Inside by the blazing fire
A loveable cat
Purrs in her sleep.

Outside in the cold winter's air
A lonely horse
Stands in the field.

Up in the tall branches
A caring mother
Is keeping her chicks warm.

Below the bare trees
A creepy spider
Is making its web.

Claire Garley (10)
Leighfield Primary School, Oakham

FIREWORKS

Catherine wheels fizz
Shooting stars sparkle
Rockets race
It's Bonfire Night.

Bangers bang
Poppers pop
Roman candles roar
It's Bonfire Night.

People scream
Dark sky
Whizzers whiz
It's Bonfire Night.

Bethany McGarrick (9)
Leighfield Primary School, Oakham

CHRISTMAS

This is what Christmas is all about.

Santa's sleigh
Flies far away.
Christmas pud
Tastes so good.
Decorative lights
Look so bright.
Busy elves
Filling shelves.
Unwrapping presents
Roasting pheasants.
Flashing red nose
Really glows.
Angels singing,
Bells ringing.
Glittering snow,
Snowman grows.
Lots of wine
Christmas time!

Ami Chapman (9)
Leighfield Primary School, Oakham

WINDY DAYS

Wind squeezes with its hands
Like elastic bands.
Wind flies about.
Wind is like a big shout.
Wind is doing bad things.
Wind knocks over dustbins.
Wind is blowing hedges.
It whistles at window ledges.
Wind is tapping kids.
Wind is snapping twigs.

Wind rushes
As he ruins bushes.
Wind hides on roofs
As he jabs horses' hooves.
Wind climbs up trees
And turns into a breeze.
Wind bites with its teeth.
Wind hides beneath.

Lucy Beardmore-Gray (8)
Leighfield Primary School, Oakham

COUNTDOWN TO BEDTIME

The sea is waving,
Look at the sun,
Moon is bright,
Number one.

The sea is waving,
Fish sewing through,
Ship goes by
Number two.

Sun glows orange,
Lovely day for me,
Drifting clouds,
Number three.

The moon shines bright,
Brighter than before,
Twinkling stars,
Number four.

End of this day,
In our beds we dive,
See you tomorrow,
One, two, three, four, five.

Rachelle Bartlett (10)
Leighfield Primary School, Oakham

SPELL OF DEATH

Double, double, toil and trouble
Fire burn and cauldron bubble . . .

Eye of rat,
Screech of cat.
Old school dinners,
Winter shivers.
Pant of dog,
Leg of frog.
Monster slime.
Vomit and grime,
Smell of blood,
Whisper of wood,
Medusa's snakes
Evil of lakes.
Horse's toe,
Cursed snow,
Heart of deer,
Every fear.
Tongue of louse
Kiss of mouse.

Now let Matefican work its magic
The consequences will be tragic.

Ally Gibson (9)
Leighfield Primary School, Oakham

MY SECRET!

There's something that I haven't said
That I would like to say,
The thing I'm thinking in my head
That I've kept, kept away.
I've had it hidden really well,
But now I want to share
My secret with you, yes I do
I want to and I dare!

I was skipping through the woods one day
When the sun did say goodbye
I thought, *oh God, I think I'm lost*
And I started to cry.
I wiped my tears and carried on
Hoping not to find my grave
When there it was in front of me
A big, dark, gloomy cave!

I walked on in without pausing to think,
And saw a mysterious light
'Oh dear!' I cried, 'I think I'm dead!'
I screamed with all my might!
I took deep and cleansing breaths,
I'm sure that I wept,
Towards the spooky light
I crept!

All of a sudden I got a shock
For the light was not there
My eyes can't be deceiving me
Could it have vanished into thin air?
Oh my gosh, it's there again.
As golden as the sun
Rounder than a bouncy ball
I thought I might have fun!

I got back home
I really hoped,
All would be fine
Oh yes, I coped.
Being in the dark
Is fun
When you've got
A ball of sun!

What's that knocking
On my door?
It's a news reporter,
Oh gosh, there's more.
I guess they've heard,
Our conversation,
I shouldn't have talked so loud,
Because now I've told the nation!

Katherine Raynes (11)
Leighfield Primary School, Oakham

HOLOCAUST

H   appy were our lives before the Nazis came.
O   bey them? We had no choice.
L   osses were numerous when we were driven into the cramped
     ghettos.
O   ur lives were no longer our own.
C   attle trucks came to carry us away.
A   drift we were, helpless in the cruel waters of their hatred.
U   tter despair filled our hearts at the sight of our evil destination.
S   tarved and tormented we gave up all hope.
T   hen the Americans came, and the torture was over.

William Broughton (11)
Leighfield Primary School, Oakham

ANGRY WIND

The wind roars.
It pours down at you.
The wind groans,
In funny tones.
The wind cracks,
And attacks really fast.
The wind blows,
And flows through your veins.
The wind gusts,
And flusters me.
The wind wrestles,
And hassles.
The wind flies,
Then dies.

Sam Tipper (8)
Leighfield Primary School, Oakham

WITHOUT YOU
(To my best friend)

Without you I'm like
A rubber with no bend
A pond with no air
Or a story with no end.

Without you I'm like
A beat with no band
A person with no friend
For whatever I do
You always understand.

Christie Clark (8)
Manor Way Primary School, Halesowen

KITTEN

A cotton ball
A miaowing powder puff
It is a cotton cushion
It is a leg warmer for wintry nights
It is a miaowing car engine.

Hope Bell (10)
Manor Way Primary School, Halesowen

A KITTEN IS A . . .

A kitten is a comfy white mitten
A kitten is a fluffy teddy
A kitten is a purring piece of cotton wool
A kitten is a fluffy ball
A miaowing powder puff.

Natalie Rogers (10)
Manor Way Primary School, Halesowen

GINGER KITTY

A kitten is a fluffy ball
A miaowing powder puff
A clawing fluffy pom-pom
A ball of cotton wool
A ball of silky fur.

Stephanie Sekula (11)
Manor Way Primary School, Halesowen

A METAPHOR POEM

A kitten is a fluffy ball
A miaowing powder puff
A kitten's purr is a motorbike
A kitten is a warm cushion
A kitten is a friend forever!

Kirsty Underhill (10)
Manor Way Primary School, Halesowen

A METAPHOR POEM

A kitten is a fluffy ball
A miaowing powder puff
A kitten is a leg warmer
A kitten is a playful football
A kitten's purr is a rustling engine.

Rachael Holloway (10)
Manor Way Primary School, Halesowen

KITTENS

A kitten is a fluffy ball
A miaowing powder puff
A kitten is a piece of dust
A miaowing ball of wool
The purr of a zooming motorbike.

Terri Gutteridge (10)
Manor Way Primary School, Halesowen

I SAW A JOLLY SURFER
(Based on 'I Saw A Jolly Hunter' by Charles Causley)

I saw a jolly surfer
On the jolly sea
Looking jolly happy
Drinking jolly tea.

He saw a jolly shark
By a jolly boat
With a jolly sailor on
In a jolly coat.

He saw a jolly pirate ship
On his jolly board
With a jolly pirate on
With a jolly sword.

Alex Holloway (9)
Manor Way Primary School, Halesowen

WITHOUT YOU
(To my best friend)

Without you I'm like
a hedgehog without prickles
a wolf without teeth
a child without nickels.

Without you I'm like
a sandpit without sand
for whatever you do
I will always understand.

Sam Jones (9)
Manor Way Primary School, Halesowen

I SAW A JOLLY PIRATE

(Based on 'I Saw A Jolly Hunter' by Charles Causley)

I saw a jolly pirate
With a jolly sword
Eating jolly birdies
He was jolly bored.

The jolly pirate
Had a jolly parrot
The jolly parrot was
Chewing on a jolly carrot.

He saw a jolly whale
In the jolly sea
He jolly gobble gobbled
He gobbled up jolly me.

Michael Williams (8)
Manor Way Primary School, Halesowen

WITHOUT YOU

(To my best friend)

Without you I'm like . . .
A wood without trees
Like a pond without fish
Like honey without bees.

Without you I'm like
A trumpet with no band
For you're always there
To hold my hand.

Roberta Hayes (8)
Manor Way Primary School, Halesowen

RED

Red is the colour of a red, red rose,
Red is the colour of the sunset or
Red is the colour of your hot, sticky toes.

Red is a big bold colour,
Lovely, jolly, happy red,
But when you're angry,
Red runs through your head.

Red is the brightest
It's higher than all,
It's like the roundest, bounciest,
Big red ball.

Thomas Stanley (9)
Manor Way Primary School, Halesowen

WITHOUT YOU
(To my best friend)

Without you I'm like,
A fish on dry land,
A rocket with no flame,
Or a beach with no sand.

Without you I'm like,
An arm with no hand
For whatever I do
You always understand.

Nicolle Birkin (9)
Manor Way Primary School, Halesowen

THE SURFER
(Based on 'I Saw A Jolly Hunter' by Charles Causley)

I saw a jolly surfer
In the jolly sea
Saw a jolly shark
Looking right at me.

I zoomed off feeling jolly scared
Got on jolly beach
Saw a jolly fisherman
Eating jolly peach.

Got back on jolly board
Went out at jolly sea
Saw jolly shark again
Ate jolly me!

Tom King (9)
Manor Way Primary School, Halesowen

WITHOUT YOU
(To my best friend)

Without you I'm like
A door that won't shut
A kangaroo without jump
Scissors that won't cut.

Without you I'm like
A fish on dry land!
For you're always there
And you will always understand.

Jenna Crompton (8)
Manor Way Primary School, Halesowen

THE JOLLY FOOTBALLER
(Based on 'I Saw A Jolly Hunter' by Charles Causley)

I saw a jolly footballer
On a jolly pitch
Running jolly round
Fell in jolly ditch.

On a jolly day
He saw a jolly mole
He had a jolly fit
And he scored a jolly goal.

Dribbled up to jolly goal
Took one jolly shoot
The jolly ball went flying
And so did his jolly boot.

Paige Walsh (8)
Manor Way Primary School, Halesowen

TOMMY BITES HIS NAILS

Tommy bit his nails all day
'Stop it you idiot!' his Mom would say
He chewed and chewed
Until he had no nails left
He chewed and chewed but
Still he kept
Biting his fingers away
And he ate his hands and arms today.

Thomas Shakespeare (9)
Manor Way Primary School, Halesowen

THE JOLLY PIRATE
(Based on 'I Saw A Jolly Hunter' by Charles Causley)

I saw a jolly pirate
On the jolly sea
With his jolly sword
Drinking jolly tea

Opened his jolly chest
Filled with jolly gold
It was jolly shiny
And it was jolly cold.

He saw a jolly whale
In the jolly sea
Squirting jolly water
At jolly frightened me.

Michael Bradshaw (9)
Manor Way Primary School, Halesowen

WITHOUT YOU
(To my best friend)

Without you I'm like . . .
a house with no bricks
a spring with no bounce
or a band with no flicks.

Without you I'm like a
duck on dry land but
whatever I do you'll
always understand.

Ryan Firman (8)
Manor Way Primary School, Halesowen

WITHOUT YOU
(To my best friend)

Without you I'm like . . .
a tree without a bark
a flower without a stem
or an alley that's not dark.

Without you I'm like . . .
a city with no street
a fox with no fur
a robin that never tweets.

Without you I'm like . . .
a tiger without stripes
for whatever Pokèmon I talk about
you always know the types.

Justin Stinson (8)
Manor Way Primary School, Halesowen

MOLLY MESS

Molly's room was in a mess
She always wore a flowery dress.
But one day her homework she had lost
'Find it now!' her mother bossed.
The teacher's name was Mr Wayne
Messy Molly got the cane.

Ben Fox (8)
Manor Way Primary School, Halesowen

WITHOUT YOU
(To my best friend)

Without you I'm like . . .
a bike without wheels
a radiator without heat
or a human without heels.

Without you I'm like . . .
a computer without memory
a house without bricks
or a CD that's temporary.

Without you I'm like . . .
a volcano without rock
a firework without a flare
or a gate without a lock.

Without you I'm like
a beach without sand
for whatever I do
you always take a stand.

James Bayley (9)
Manor Way Primary School, Halesowen

LIZZY LITTER

Lizzy was a lovely lass
She was skipping on the grass
She dropped some litter on the ground
Just then a man passed by, caught her by his eye
He told her off and made her cry.

James Dwyer (9)
Manor Way Primary School, Halesowen

164

WITHOUT YOU
(To my best friend)

Without you I'm like a house without a TV.
Without you I'm like a field without a tree.
Without you I'm like a key without a lock.
Without you I'm like a bird without wings.

Without you I'm like a car without a door,
Without you I'm like a fish out of water,
Without you I'm like a nurse without a medical kit,
Without you I'm like a dog without a bark.

Without you I'm like a cat without a mouse,
Without you I'm like a whale that can't swim,
Without you I'm like a teacher without a class.

Without you I'm lost.

Rhea Smith (9)
Manor Way Primary School, Halesowen

HAIR-CHEWING ROBERTA

Roberta's hair was very long,
She only did one thing wrong,
She chewed her hair all day,
She was poorly and couldn't play,
So her mom cut her hair,
Then her head was cold and bare.

Rosie Adams (9)
Manor Way Primary School, Halesowen

I SAW A JOLLY FOOTBALLER

(Based on 'I Saw A Jolly Hunter' by Charles Causley)

I saw a jolly footballer
On the jolly pitch
Running jolly round
With a jolly stitch.

I saw a jolly match
With a jolly crowd
Old jolly Zola
Was jolly proud.

I saw a jolly ref
With a jolly whistle
Fell in a jolly bush
Which was a jolly thistle.

Michael Topping (9)
Manor Way Primary School, Halesowen

WITHOUT YOU

(To my best friend)

Without you I'm like . . .
A sun without light
A cat without fur
Or a ghost without fright.

Without you I'm like . . .
A teddy where no one holds it tight
A world that is damp and dark
An animal that no one likes.

Bethany Thompson (8)
Manor Way Primary School, Halesowen

WITHOUT YOU
(To my best friend)

Without you I'm like
a fire without heat
a ship without a sail
a heart without a beat.

Without you I'm like
a fox without a tail
or a snake without a hiss
or a sea without a whale.

Without you I'm like
a fingerless hand,
For, whatever I do I know
You always understand.

Rose Goldman (9)
Manor Way Primary School, Halesowen

HUNGRY, LONELY, SCARED

Sitting in the darkness thinking of my mom,
Hungry, lonely, scared, whatever shall I do now?

Sweet and tender Mom would not fit in this
Ebony dark place,
Hungry, lonely, scared, whatever shall I do now?

Touching the bumpy cold wall makes me shiver with fear,
Hungry, lonely, scared, whatever shall I do now?

Sitting in the darkness thinking of my mom,
Hungry, lonely, scared, whatever shall I do now?

Tiffany Johnstone (8)
Mount Pleasant Primary School, Brierley Hill

MY ADVERBIAL POEM

Friendly
The small young boy
Helped his mate up.

Astonishingly
Baby animals develop
From their mums.

Intricately
The world is made.

Elegantly
The man stepped forward
Step by step.

Thankfully
The tall, gentle, smart boy
Thanked the man.

Priyesh Patel (8)
Mount Pleasant Primary School, Brierley Hill

UNTITLED

As I sit deeply in my corner in the damp wet mine
I miss my mother, everyday I think of my mother's beautiful face.

I am sitting heartbroken in front of a door
When it opens the black tunnel embraces me.

The biting door rips my fingers apart.

I want to go home but I cannot,
It's like a curse to make me stay here.

Josh Lambe (9)
Mount Pleasant Primary School, Brierley Hill

DREADFUL LIFE!

I sit, waiting, lonely, hurt inside,
Outside the sun is shining but just look at me,
Terrible,
I could die of many different things!
It seems like days, weeks, but I've only been
Here three hours.
Four carts have already crushed my dark, dirty skin,
Save me, help me,
I'm hungry and cold,
The darkness bullies me, not from sounds but looks!
And then a real noise in the distance,
The door handle has disappeared,
I've missed my chance,
Now I've been crushed five times!
Dripping down on me is a leak,
A leak no one cares about,
A leak that can join my sad tears.
Every now and then someone will come
And tell me how stupid I am.
But no one cares! I think,
You can tell!
Always night down here, never daytime here!
The boring black walls stare at me,
I want to go to sleep,
I hope I don't!
This is my life, what a dreadful life!
Mother, Father, come and rescue me from this vile place
Get me out of here, my life depends on it.

Georgia Williams (8)
Mount Pleasant Primary School, Brierley Hill

DOES ANYBODY KNOW WHO I AM?

Kneeling down in my dark damp space,
My grazed skin all scratched and bruised,
Cold and lonely,
Starving and thirsty,
Does anybody know where I am?

The bumping and rattling of the wooden carts,
Running slowly across the rails that
Nearly crush me as I wait.
Cold and lonely,
Starving and thirsty,
Does anybody know who I am?

Pictures come to mind of when I was younger,
Mom, Dad, my brother and me,
Playing together all day long,
But now,
Cold and lonely,
Starving and thirsty,
Does anybody care where I am?

Nobody knows how I feel,
Even if I told anyone nobody would care,
Always scared of carts hitting me,
Tired from no sleep,
Cold and lonely,
Starving and thirsty,
Does anybody care who I am?
Praying now all day long,
Wishing that one day someone will come,
Take me home,
In the warm,
Cold and lonely,
Starving and thirsty,
Does anybody know where I am?

Bethany-Rose Madkins (9)
Mount Pleasant Primary School, Brierley Hill

DOWN IN THE MINE

There I sit in a dark and gloomy cramped space
Day and night, with no food.

I'm hungry, I'm starving,
I miss my mom and dad.

I'm poorly, I don't like working down
In the mine.

I'm dirty, smelly, poorly,
Please let me go home.

My mom and dad, my brother and sister
Are missing me at the moment.

I'm hungry, I'm starving,
I miss my mom and dad.

Lily Staves (8)
Mount Pleasant Primary School, Brierley Hill

THE MINES

I'm alone in the cold, dark mines.
I hear the coal tub come,
I open the door as wide as I can.
The coal tub passes by as it makes a rumbling noise
As it comes.
I'm hungry, I can only dream of being with my family
By the warm and comfortable fire.
Alone. Does anyone care?
Does anyone come to me?
Alone in the mysterious darkness.

Rikesh Patel (9)
Mount Pleasant Primary School, Brierley Hill

MINE POEM

Sitting in the dark
There's no light.

Nobody to hold me tight,
As a thumping sound comes nearer and nearer,
I grasp my hands tightly together
Thinking of my mother in the warm that's kind.

One day, just maybe, I'll get to see and be part of a family,
Please help me, oh please!
I'm scared, scared as you can be.

It's cold and damp, very cold and damp,
Men walk by looking at me! Why oh why?
Don't ask me!

Simone Round *(9)*
Mount Pleasant Primary School, Brierley Hill

THE DARK MINES

As I sit alone thinking about my mother at home
I wish she was here with me every night and day
It's not fair
This dark and horrible place is making me not care.

I try to escape but the only way out is the gate.
Hearing coal carts pass me by
It seems like I'm in prison.

Shardae McDonald *(9)*
Mount Pleasant Primary School, Brierley Hill

THE POOR AND LONELY CHILD

In pitch-black mines time goes by.
Never knowing if it's dark or light,
No food, no drink, no nothing.
My feet bleed by sharp stones and rocks
Rocky walls hard as can be.

While working I cry my eyes out.
Wishing and wishing, waiting until the day comes
When I can be free from the cold and dark mines
Where I freeze.
It will never come.

I open the doors whenever the cars, that are like monsters
To me, come by.
When I close my eyes it is black, and when I open them
It is still black.
I'm scared stiff in the cold.
No lights.

No one cares, no one is friendly,
My mother might be missing me.
I'm missing her too.
I wonder what is happening at home.

Kate Adams (9)
Mount Pleasant Primary School, Brierley Hill

COLD, DARK, DULL

Cold, dark, dull,
If it was up to me I wouldn't be here
But I have to for my family.

My job is to push the giant black coal trucks
Straining and hurting my muscles
Cold, dark, dull.

The early years of my life,
I spent on land,
But now the only thing for me is endless
Darkness and cold chill.
Cold, dark, dull.

For me there's only night there's never any light.
Cold, dark, dull.

Ben Carrington (9)
Mount Pleasant Primary School, Brierley Hill

MINE LIFE

In the mine I stare into darkness,
I pull open the door for the pushers,
Does anybody know I'm here?
I have often had my toes and feet hurt
As the carts are pushed onto me.
This place is far from comfortable.
As I sit in this dreadful pit I wonder if I will
Ever see daylight again,
I wish my parents would give me my pennies for school.

Ryan North (9)
Mount Pleasant Primary School, Brierley Hill

TIME GOES BY

Deep in my space the loaded trucks forwards,
Closer to me.
I am worried, I am starving
Time goes by.
Missing my father and mother, I scramble to open the door.
Scared, lonely, starving.
Time goes by.
Cold as a winter's day, I shake every second,
Coughing.
Starving as time goes by.
My family and I would be playing happily,
I guess not now.
Cold, lonely, starving.
Time goes by.
Now I am alone, deep in my space
The loaded trucks race towards me as
Time goes by.
I want somebody to love me,
I want somebody to care.
I guess nobody knows me
I guess they wouldn't dare.
Cold, lonely, starving.
Time goes by.

Katie North (9)
Mount Pleasant Primary School, Brierley Hill

DOWN THE MINE

The dark from down below
Coal trucks thunder past
No food, no light.
My family are nowhere in sight
Touching those walls of dust
No food, no light.
Sitting still on rocks so sharp
Pushing, pulling, creaky doors.
No food, no light.
No one cares, I'm alone, in the dark.
Lonely, sad, so lonely.
Missing my days in sunlight.
Now my days are in darkness.
My friends are far, far away
No food, no light.
Before I know it I'll die
I'm thinking I'm going to survive.

Liam Bradley (8)
Mount Pleasant Primary School, Brierley Hill

ALONE IN THE DARK

A little boy waiting patiently down the mine
Trucks rumbling by.
The doors are opened as the trucks go by.
Coughing loudly as the trucks go thundering on.
Dust coming off the trucks.
Sitting dozing off by the locks.
He wished his mother and father were there.
He is living in darkness, it is cold.
He is frightened as he sits in the corner.
He was shaking in the corner.

Louise Pinnell (9)
Mount Pleasant Primary School, Brierley Hill

DOWN IN THE DARK MINES

I have no bones left,
The people that die,
My friends who have got loads of dust
Over them,
I dream of my mom and dad being here with me.
It is really sunny outside,
We never are allowed outside,
We just have to keep working,
So please be near to my mom and dad
And I will always love them to bits.
I don't know why I have to work down here.

It feels like my mom used to come down to the mine,
She always used to say when I was with her 'I love you.'

They used to say 'It is good to crush your bones,
It will not make you strong.'

Does anybody care about me?
I'm hungry, does anybody care?

Daniel Appleton (8)
Mount Pleasant Primary School, Brierley Hill

ALONE IN THE DARK

Here I sit in the cold, dark, scary mine
Thinking and dreaming of my mom and dad.
Nobody cares, nobody worries, nobody thinks about me.
I hear rattling of the cart so I push myself against the wall.
When the cart is here, I curl up so I can't get crushed.

Nobody cares, nobody worries, nobody thinks about me.

Laura Taylor (8)
Mount Pleasant Primary School, Brierley Hill

ME IN THE MINE

Me in the mine, dark and quiet
I'm thinking of my mom's face when she's crying.
I'm very scared.
I am thinking of my mom in the dark waiting for me
To come home.
I am really scared of the dark.
The cart is coming,
I can't open the door.
At last I opened it in time!
I wish my mom and dad and brother were here to help me.
I try to escape but I can't
It's like I'm in prison.
At last the clock strikes twelve.
I go home.
I hug my mom when I got home.
My mom says, 'You are safe here now.'

Amie Adams (8)
Mount Pleasant Primary School, Brierley Hill

RIGHT - WRITE!

If you write with your right, you're right
You're right in your test,
When you write with your right,
But if you go left,
When you write with your left,
You'll still be right without
Writing with your right.

Sasha Guest (10)
Mount Pleasant Primary School, Brierley Hill

ALONE IN THE MINE

Deep in the darkness of the dripping mine,
Lonely, starving and cold.
Alone in the darkness as time passes.

As I sit down I dream about my mum and dad.
Starving, lonely and scared alone in the dripping darkness
Leaning against the wall.

Standing against the wall I hear a cart of coal
Rattling down the rails.
I know I have to open the door then I stand back
And watch the cart go past.
I shut the door and stand back again.

I stand there wishing I could have some light and food.
I cannot stop thinking about my family
How they are coping outside of the mine.

Matthew Reese (8)
Mount Pleasant Primary School, Brierley Hill

EGYPTIANS

E   gypt is an historical place
G   iant pyramids stand full of grace
Y   ou will never want to leave
P   haraohs keep you there with ease
T   utankhamen lies still in his tomb
I   wonder if he'll ever be moved
A   mazing wonders of the world
N   ever should this land be disturbed
S   un is shining on the sand reflecting off this wonderful land.

Alison Clarke (10)
Mount Pleasant Primary School, Brierley Hill

IN THE MINES

Deep, black, scary mines down in the darkness, all the time.
No food, no home and coal rushing past me all the time.
I think about my mother all the time.
Being loved, every day, scared, no light.
I hear bangs day by day.
Hard, rocky walls hurt all day long.
Tripping on the stones surrounding the ground.
Crying, no one with me
Lonely, worried and upset.

Down in the darkness on my own
Cold, freezing and dirty.
No one to speak to.
I want to be out of the mines.
Step by step I'm in the mines forever.

Jasmine Worsfold (9)
Mount Pleasant Primary School, Brierley Hill

THE CYCLE BEGINS

Trickling tributaries winding wilfully downhill
Splashing stream streaking silently onwards
Lazy lakes lying listlessly
Whooshing waterfalls bravely bombarding the river below
Rising into raging rivers rushing, rampaging
Swelling into sparkly, salty, supreme seas.
        Rivers!

Jordan Madkins (10)
Mount Pleasant Primary School, Brierley Hill

DOWN IN THE DEEP BLACK MINES

Thinking deeply of my mother's sweet, bright face,
When carts are pulled onto me and make me have a brace.

A cloud of black smoke makes me cough
And stops me thinking of my mother.

The smoke was a warning sign
As the cart is pulled onto me.

Bones are broken,
Fingers have come off,
Blood is pouring out of me.

I use my last bit of strength to open the door
For the other carts.

I wonder when I will be able to see my mother
And father again.

Michael Pearson (9)
Mount Pleasant Primary School, Brierley Hill

GOD'S GIFT OF FOOD

Harvest is a joyous time
All the crops in little heaps
And brown potatoes in small mounds.

Together God and farmers work,
For God's almighty hand fed and watered the land.

The year is over, harvest is collected
The year is over, harvest is eaten.

Charlotte Prosser (11)
Mount Pleasant Primary School, Brierley Hill

DREAMS

As I was walking in thick fog
I tripped and fell upon a log.
Before my eyes a man appeared
Two big circles a long white beard.

I felt my heart miss a beat
As I tried to scramble to my feet,
The ground beneath me was covered in mud,
I felt a trickle of wet, cold blood.

I managed to get back on my feet
My heart was pounding fast and deep
I ran and ran as fast as I could
Jumping and leaping over rocks and wood.

I felt so scared and started to shout.
I turned over and began to wake.
All this was only a dream
I'm so glad I didn't scream.

Kirsty Tolley (11)
Mount Pleasant Primary School, Brierley Hill

THE HARVEST

H   is for harvest, which comes every year
A   is for abundance we collect our food of plenty
R   is for rain, which makes the crops grow
V   is for vegetables, which we share at harvest
E   is for eating, for when the harvest's over
S   is for sowing, to start the process all over again
T   is for turnips, turnips are very good for harvests.

Stephanie Wheeldon (10)
Mount Pleasant Primary School, Brierley Hill

CAR ATTACK

On last year's Hallowe'en
A car hit Auntie Jean.
Unhinged by this attack
My auntie hit it back.

She hit it with her handbag
And knocked it with her knee,
She socked it with a sandbag,
And thumped it with a tree.

On last year's Hallowe'en
A car hit Auntie Jean,
And now, my auntie's better
But the car is with the wrecker.

Jodie Cox (10)
Mount Pleasant Primary School, Brierley Hill

THE SEA

The sea is as blue as a glistening sapphire,
The sea is as hot as a warm, soothing bath.
The sea is a pool of Turkish green stones.
The sea is a sky-blue, greenish colour.
The sea is as clear as a window to another world.
The sea is a pure jewel.
The sea is as cold as ice.
The sea is as cold and as freezing as an iceberg.
The sea is as fast as a leopard.
The sea is as calm as a summer's day.
The sea is as rough as the howling wind.
The sea is as shimmering as a shooting star.
I love the sea.
The sea is all of these.

Rebecca Hemmings (11)
Mount Pleasant Primary School, Brierley Hill

RESOLUTION

R eady to run away from your fears
   no worries, no tears
E veryone enjoys the time of their lives
   and fills their hearts with pride
S uper things will happen right now,
   it is not the time to have a row
O nly try better in helping everyone
L ead your life with a new leaf
   Turn it over and you will see a new beginning
   to your life
U ntil your life will go away, it will erase the
   memories that you had before
T errible things have happened in the past,
   you will see how quickly they pass.
I nteresting things have lasted so well
O nly you can think of your new resolution
N estled safely in your mind.

Elisha Caldwell (11)
Mount Pleasant Primary School, Brierley Hill

BIRTHDAY

Beginning the day bright and early
It's my birthday hip hip hooray!
Ready to collect the post,
There on the mat, who has the most.
Hooray, it's birthday cards for me,
Ding-dong, goes the doorbell,
And there stands the postman,
'Your birthday young man,' as he hands me a parcel.

Robert Bloomer (10)
Mount Pleasant Primary School, Brierley Hill

MEMORIAL GARDEN

Water trickles down the fountain
You can hear the brilliant birds
Singing a tune.
The aroma of freshly grown flowers fills the air.
In summer.

Snow glistens on the fountain holding the water prisoner.
There is very little wildlife on the pebbles and plants anymore
Except two little squirrels scampering for food.
In winter.

Rain splatters against the smooth pebbles,
Just missing the squirrels.
Leaves are crunchy underfoot
Once the leaves start to drop,
They never stop.
In autumn.

Raindrops travel down the side of the fountain.
Leaves re-grow and soon will be magnificent trees.
Tree buds will blossom and will be brightly coloured flowers.
In spring.

Laura Banks (11)
Mount Pleasant Primary School, Brierley Hill

THE FOREST

Treetops sway in the fresh air that blows the sizzling red leaves
off the broken branches.

Howling noisily from the top of his voice the sly, ebony fox
prowls around late at night.

Evergreen grass sways in the air,
as the beautiful birds sing in the chunky trees.

Falling and swirling to the gravelly ground,
the crunchy leaves create a tornado floating above the land.

Overlooking the dazzling hills you can see trickles of rainwater
floating above the snowy clouds.

Roaring and racing, rapidly the river splashes the overgrowth
entwining itself together.

Everywhere all over the land sneaky animals climb from tree to tree
and stroll on the ground.

Sloths swiftly slide up the chunky trees in the daylight.

Tropical, tall trees grow silently in the refreshing atmosphere.

Kirstie Taylor (10)
Mount Pleasant Primary School, Brierley Hill

THE SNOWY RABBIT

I love Peter Rabbit
His coat is as white as snow
He follows me everywhere I go.

I love Peter Rabbit
His fur is soft and fluffy
He growls like a dog
He headbutts our neighbour Duffy.

I love Peter Rabbit
He jumps like a deer
But he doesn't like a beer.

I love Peter Rabbit
He has floppy ears
And drives my mom into tears
When he digs up the garden.

Stacey Crook (11)
Mount Pleasant Primary School, Brierley Hill

THE FOOTBALLING WORLD

The footballing world, such a delight,
A player sprinting down the wing to hit the ball into the net,
He scores a goal, the fans scream
Goal!
The fans go wild in all countries including the Premier League,
Also La Liga the Spanish League and all other countries.
The footballing world and competitions started over one hundred
years ago, and thereon the matches have been so exciting.
The footballing world a great place to be.

Kristopher Fellows (10)
Mount Pleasant Primary School, Brierley Hill

FOOTBALL CRAZY

Fantastically,
I won the match
I was proud
To score a goal.

Thankfully
My dad got me tickets
To a football match.

Kindly
David Beckham
Gave me
His autograph.

Magically
Football crazy
Came on
And I joined in.

Samuel Freestone (8)
Mount Pleasant Primary School, Brierley Hill

BLUE

B   is for blue the colour of the sky on a hot exotic day
L   is for love which I feel for my family
U   is for umbrella which is used a lot in the UK
E   is for energy which is provided by the juice drink . . .
    Lucozade.

Faye Bradley (11)
Mount Pleasant Primary School, Brierley Hill

THE SEA STORM

One day out of my window,
I saw the deep blue sea.
It passed beyond the cliffs,
And then it passed in front of me.
But the sea helps explorers.

Sometimes the sea can be vicious,
When it smashes against rocks,
I compare this to
Some locomotive steam cocks.
But the sea helps explorers.

Sometimes the sea can be like a relaxing bath,
As it gently passes by.
But there is one thing to remember,
The sea will never die.
But the sea helps explorers.

When the sea is calm,
It's time for the sailors to start.
But one of the sailors could be,
The great master of art.

Daniel Such (10)
Mount Pleasant Primary School, Brierley Hill

THE PHARAOH IN THE AFTER LIFE

I am the once powerful Pharaoh Snerferu,
Mummified and buried.
Once I felt the set of sun,
Now I have been humbled.
The crown once placed upon my head,
Now sits upon my son.

Five days past after my ceremony,
I ejected from my body.
I rose up to the heavens,
Welcomed by a bright flash.

I was given a warm greeting,
By the humble god Anubis.
He took me to the great hall,
For which I had been dreaming of.
My heart was weighed against a feather
The symbol of two truths.
My heart was a worthy opponent,
And passed to the next world.

After many centuries,
In the land of the gods,
I began to feel hunted,
By mortals down on Earth.

Soon after I heard this disturbing news,
In my heavenly home.
I went back down to my resting place,
To find my body gone.

After many days searching,
I finally found my remains,
In a glass case,
On display to the public.
A museum not a pyramid,
Was now my home!

Aaron Chawro (11)
Mount Pleasant Primary School, Brierley Hill

ALL ABOUT MY TWO PEOPLE

Look at the man
Pull a face
Then the man looks
And he starts to chase.

The man ran fast
The boy ran slow
The man caught him
And the boy said, 'Hello.'

The man was amazed
At what he had seen
The boy was cross
That the man was mean.

Don't pull faces
At strange old men
Because they may chase you
To their den.

Thomas Taylor (7)
Mount Pleasant Primary School, Brierley Hill

PICTURE OF WORDS

Kindly,
Helping my friend
Pick up snowballs
While it crunches
Under my feet.

Happily,
I played in the garden
While the snowflakes
Fall from the roof
To the green.

Thankfully,
I got what I wanted
When I immediately
Went to bed.
I found it in my dreams.

Gracefully,
I galloped
Through the field
On my clean
Black horse.

Carefully
I made a
Magical toy
That glistened
Through every window.

Louisa Hampson *(7)*
Mount Pleasant Primary School, Brierley Hill

THE CARE

Gently
Floating feathers
Fall gently
Birds singing as
Beaks snap.
Carefully
Angels fly in
The sky.
Care is true.
I love you.
Beautifully
Flying birds
Fluttering in the sky.
Pretty girls dancing
Like dancing queens.
Friendly
Happy people
Jumping around.
Friends helping
Each other.
Kindly
Fairies flapping
Around the lights,
Care is around us
Like a sun in the sky.

Bethany Smith   (8)
Mount Pleasant Primary School, Brierley Hill

Daniel's Adverbial Poem

Gracefully
As I saw a bird fly by
With its elegant wings flapping
I thought of
Fluffy clouds.

I see a beautiful
Young girl
Holding hands gently
With a little child.

Pleasingly
A mother
Gives her child
A special gift
Of some sort.

I would give
All I could
To help
A friend in need.

I watch a swift pile of leaves
Float down and down until
They hit the green.

Daniel Layland (7)
Mount Pleasant Primary School, Brierley Hill

WEIRD MAGIC

Friendly
Friends are
Helpful,
Friends are
Smart and cool!

Gently
The flowers
Glided in the wind's
Beautiful breeze.

Dizzily
I fell over
On the floor
When I was dizzy
Like a spinning top.

Magically
We disappear like a
Bunny that's being stuffed
Into a top hat.

Incredibly
Shooting stars
Shoot past the moon
At the speed of light.

Connor Brinsdon (7)
Mount Pleasant Primary School, Brierley Hill

THE SEASONS OF POEMS

Friendly
Friends who care
Friends who like you
Friends who play with you all night
Friends with lots of joy
And friends who share.

Fantastically
The stars are twinkling
The moon is bright
The sun is happy
With all its might
Clouds are fluffy like little kittens.

Delicately
The glass reflecting
Icicles sparkling
Snowflakes dripping
And falling from the sky.

Kindly
Sharing your beautiful work
Shining and stunning
The work looking back at us
The work for all to see.

Happily
The boys and girls
Come out to play
Leaving their beds they creep
Moon shining bright as day.

Danielle Baker (8)
Mount Pleasant Primary School, Brierley Hill

DELICATE POEMS

Beautifully
Colourful butterflies
Flew gently
To the cold
And frosty ground.

Delicately
Cold snowflakes
Fall down
Past the
Elegant butterfly.

Kindly
People
Playing gently
With each other.

Carelessly
Broken heart
Could be shattered
Just by one word.

Carefully
Raindrops slide off roofs
And fall down pipes
As fast as a car.

Kate Paynter (7)
Mount Pleasant Primary School, Brierley Hill

MY ADVERBIAL POEM

Gracefully,
The amazing
Dove glided
Through the never-ending
Azure sky.

Delicately
The pure
Water flows
Down the winding lake.

Astonishingly
The snowflakes
Fall slowly
Onto the towering tree.

Carefully
The graceful
Baby swan
Pursued his
Mother and father.

The friendly
Hedgehog crawled
Through the bushes
As delicately
As a spider.

Adam Lambe *(7)*
Mount Pleasant Primary School, Brierley Hill

THE WORLD

Wonderfully
The snowflakes fall onto the treetops
Leaving nothing at all
Only the fingerprints
Of the white snow.

Gracefully
Children dance
Pointing their toes
Around the open fire
Dancing using gradual music.

Beautifully
The flowers grow small like pansies, roses
And lilies just appear in thin air
I wonder if it's God or water
I wonder if it's me helping it.

Fantastically
Stars twinkle
In the night to find that in the morning
They are gone
The stars sparkle in the moonlight.

Carelessly
Broken hearts are gone forever
To never come back till Valentine's
Till 3002 when Valentine's Day has gone
Please let us get a new heart.

Gemma Raybould (8)
Mount Pleasant Primary School, Brierley Hill

THE WORLD

Carelessly,
A poor heart is
Broken from
Painful words and
A break up.

Fantastically,
A worm does
A twist in a
Very outstanding
Way.

Gracefully,
Butterflies flutter
Around flowers
Slowly
From side to side.

Happily,
Friends play together
With other people too
Tag tag
You're it.

Beautifully,
Stars shoot
Up with glitter falling
Then light up the dark, dark sky
From one end to the other.

Olivia Fullwood (8)
Mount Pleasant Primary School, Brierley Hill

TRAVELLER AND SPIRITS

In the dark, spooky, silent forest,
Only a twig snap could break the stillness
But then a foot, a hoof came along
A crack, a creak and then . . .
Someone shouted and knocked . . .

The voice questioned,
'Is there anyone there?'
No answer, it's failed
He turned around and looked
He smote on the door once again.

But only a faint whistle in the distance came
A sudden shiver cooled the wood,
Just, a sudden creak
Sent a shiver up the spine
His breath went white and froze.

His eyes watered
It's twelve o'clock
But one last try and then . . .
This time something a . . .
Shriek!

Suddenly he jumped, and then turned and ran
And after that nobody ever passed that haunted house again
And nobody ever saw him again.

Krtistina Evans (9)
Mount Pleasant Primary School, Brierley Hill

THE SHIP

In a dark harbour with
Boxes and rats a sailor
Stood perplexed,
Staring at the misty ship.
This sailor was here for his night shift.

He felt the cold air whip
Across his pale face.
He could hear a group of
Phantoms,
Playing cards, climbing the rigging
And scrubbing the decks.
They started making sounds
Like a foghorn in the background.

'Can you hear me?' he said,
'Can you hear me?' and again
He said it.
But no one replied,
And still the ghouls were making
Sounds of a foghorn.
The sailor tripped and the ship sailed
Off into the dark night.

Thomas Wilkins (10)
Mount Pleasant Primary School, Brierley Hill

THE PHANTOM LISTENERS ON THE SHIP

I rowed towards an old wrecked ship,
Making splashes in the salty sea with my oars,
I reached the deserted ship and climbed over the rotten side.

The ship was dirty, disgusting and old.
I shouted out, 'Is there anyone here?'
But no one answered.
I had a feeling that some spooked-out phantom listeners
Were watching me.
I stood there silently for a few minutes
Then all of a sudden the ship gave a gigantic jolt
And then it gave a tiny shudder.

I'd had enough of this horrid spooky shaking ship
I ran to port,
Then I jumped straight off into my shiny new boat.
I went ashore to my loving housemaid
And to this day I look outside
The moonlit ship looks all alone.
I would never ever go there again.

Sarah Redding (9)
Mount Pleasant Primary School, Brierley Hill

THE SPOOKED CASTLE

The traveller knocked on the castle door
'Anybody there?'
As he spoke his voice echoed through the castle floor.

Again he knocked
'Anybody there?'
No reply.

'Hello! Anybody there?'
No one answered.
Only the phantoms were listening
But they didn't answer.

As he rode away on his golden-backed noble steed
The moon shone brightly on the castle door.
He heard something ahead
His horse walked slowly
As the horse trotted
The grass crunched softly beneath its heels.

Elyse Evers (10)
Mount Pleasant Primary School, Brierley Hill

THE GHOSTLY, GLOOMY HOUSE

The dark, hooded stranger,
Sat all alone
In the haunted, hawked wood.
Time passed, he was gone.
To the house that stood alone.
The door opened,
And there suddenly appeared a strange man.

The man dropped on the floor
Was he dead or not?
There lay the old crinkled man.
He had lost his pinkness in his face.
So by this time he was pale.

I tried talking to him,
But he just lay there.
When he could finally speak
He said, 'You want to know what went on, don't you?'
By this time he was shaking like a washing machine.

The ghosts came out,
And the traveller was as scared as a monkey being chased
But after two minutes they had disappeared
Into another world
And from this day on, he has always heard horrible noises . . .

Rebecca Godwin (10)
Mount Pleasant Primary School, Brierley Hill

THE PHANTOM SHIP

As the traveller's grey eyes gazed up and down the wrecked ship,
His long, straggly moonlit hair swayed lazily about his shoulders.
The traveller smote the ship a first time and cried,
'Is there anyone there?'
Although no one answered, he could sense a phantom presence.
Bloodthirsty, creepy creatures, hearkened to every word he spoke.
After a third knock upon the door, he cried,
'I know you're in there! Tell them I came, tell them I came!'
But before he could go anywhere . . .
The spirits came swarming in from all directions.
Suddenly horses neighed and clattered as the traveller disappeared
Into the bewitching night.
Those ghostly creatures are no longer there
But they could be here . . .

Laura Harkin (10)
Mount Pleasant Primary School, Brierley Hill

MY DREAMS

Delicately
Snowflakes fall gently
Covering the green
With pure white fingers.

Happily
The clouds gathered together
Making the sky so white
Like a small ball of
Cotton wool.

Dominic Priest (8)
Mount Pleasant Primary School, Brierley Hill

WONDERFULLY

Gracefully,
Birds fly high in the sky
Created by God
With their soft, beautiful wings
And their shiny orange beaks.

Beautifully
Dolphins swim in the deep blue sea
As they leap out of the water calling
With their outstanding voice
Communicating.

Intricately
The day follows the night
And the night follows
The day
Then the day comes to an end.

Friendly
People shout
And play games
Together
And they enjoy their time together.

Carelessly
Someone broke a heart
With nasty words.

Abbie Morgan (8)
Mount Pleasant Primary School, Brierley Hill

FANCY ADVERBS

Gracefully
Horses
Jump
Over big
Huge fences.

Gently
Someone touched a
Soft petal
Like a thin quilt.

Elegantly
Birds fly
Elegantly in the sky
Like a shooting star
Just being shot out of a cannon.

Beautiful
There are beautiful flowers
Like a rose or a daffodil.

Kindly
Someone kindly gave me
A big huge present.

Aaran Tranter (8)
Mount Pleasant Primary School, Brierley Hill

FOOTIE POEM

Fantastically
Kicking the
Speeding
Ball.

Incredibly
Like the
Speed of light
Passes the goalie.

Amazingly
Crossing the line
Nearly hitting the net.

Delicately
Football
Skimming the net
Running down to the pitch.

Magically
Winning
1-0.

Lewis Girling (8)
Mount Pleasant Primary School, Brierley Hill

MY DREAM POEM

I dream of a floating shining star above me
In my head I dream of multicoloured ribbons
Floating gently in the thin air
And angels flutter away in the sky.
I dream of flowers shooting up from the ground
I dream of pure white clouds sitting on the
Transparent air.

I dream of splashing with water when a huge
Butterfly with dazzling glitter appears,
Like sparkling sapphires coming from the sky.
Then the night falls and the sun becomes moon
And the shining brilliant stars are in the clouds.

The dark midnight sky dreaming away,
And the bright stars fade away.
The sun rises up, up and up.
The good day starts again.

Rebecca Shaw (7)
Mount Pleasant Primary School, Brierley Hill

210

MY WONDERFUL POEMS

Carefully
Delicate snowflakes
Touched the soft ground
As I walk through the amazing air
The emerald carpet turns
Glittering white.

Incredibly
The golden daylight
Shines like a shining diamond
Then it turns to night
The lovely moon appears.

Beautifully
A little seed is planted
Then it grows into a dazzling flower
It turns out to be a loving flower.

Fantastically
Heaven shines like a glamorous crystal
By a lovely silver star
Everything lights up
As a shooting star appears.

Gracefully
I see a kind dog
It is as white as a beautiful star
It looks like a snow dog
The fantastic dog sits as quiet as a mouse.

Laura Whitehead (7)
Mount Pleasant Primary School, Brierley Hill

MY DELICATE SNOW

Dizzily
I walked the amazing fields
While the delicate snow fell
Slowly to earth.

Elegantly
The field stopped
The day went by quickly
As the night moon gathered up to meet the stars
They shone beautifully in the midnight sky.

Gracefully
While the stars were in the midnight sky
The snow fell gently to the green.

Delicately
The snow patted
On the window
I woke to find a sea of
White land.

Magnificently
The snow came down
To meet the rough red leaves
And gently onto the villages
Below.

Katie-Jo Clarke (8)
Mount Pleasant Primary School, Brierley Hill

WORLD OF DREAMS

Carelessly
A broken rainbow
A cruel laugh
From high in the sky
The evil queen is there.

Friendly
Let's be friendly
Are you alone?
Come on let's play.

Kind
Let's be kind, give him a pencil
And a glue pot
Let him share that book.

Andrew Raybould (7)
Mount Pleasant Primary School, Brierley Hill

PAT THE CAT

My pet named Pat was a beautiful cat.
She sat on a mat then chased a rat.
The rat ran fast, the cat ran faster.
In the end Pat caught the rat.
The rat wiggled away, the cat went mad.
The end of this story is very sad
The rat called his friends, the cat got scared
The rats ran fast, the cat got scared.

Lorna Watts (8)
Mount Pleasant Primary School, Brierley Hill

DREAM

I had a poem
In my car.
I went to fetch it,
I left my car door ajar.

My friend had two dogs
They ran in the fog
Around the fog.

I had a dream
My sister was a queen
She is pretty
With a pretty dress.
She walked along
With pretty shoes
Singing a song.

Josie Cartwright (8)
Mount Pleasant Primary School, Brierley Hill

THE RAIN

In the rain you get wet
In the rain you have a picnic set
In the rain you might have a bet
In the rain you might have a net.
When you get in your house, you get dressed
Then you go to bed in your nightie
Wake up in the morning I sing,
'Rain, rain go away, come again another day.'

Shantelle McDonald (7)
Mount Pleasant Primary School, Brierley Hill

FET MY PET

My name is Jet
And I have a pet
Her name is Fet
And I get her to fetch.

Men can fight Fet
Men can't beat Fet
I can watch TV with Fet.

Men can dance with Fet
I can play on the computer with Fet.
I can play games with Fet
I can go swimming with Fet.

I can punish Fet
I can help Fet
I can feed Fet
Fet is my pet

   Dog!

Daniel Lander *(7)*
Mount Pleasant Primary School, Brierley Hill

MY SISTER

I had a dream
About my sister
Being a queen
With a blister.

She picked the blister
With a leg spoon
She made it bleed
What a goon.

I said, 'yuck
You are disgusting
Like the loo
Or the dustbin.'

The dream ended
All was well
My sister was alright
But she still smells.

Amelia Evers (8)
Mount Pleasant Primary School, Brierley Hill

MY WONDERFUL DREAM POEM

Thankfully the bright blue sky
Is very cloudy.
The clouds are fluffy.
The sun shines bright
Past all the sunlit sky.

Incredibly flowers and fields
Surround me happily
They take me away.

Georgina Dawes (8)
Mount Pleasant Primary School, Brierley Hill

THE SPECIAL THINGS YOU LOVE

Kindly
Stars flow top to bottom in the air,
That has a moon that smiles every day and night
And one side to another side by the stars each way.

Gently
Angels cry help while singing a wonderful song,
That touches the sun,
That drops by delight and happiness
In the dark blue sky.

Dizzily
Liquid falls like the rain is falling down
From the sky that shines down to the ground
On the touching pebbles that crush
Together on the very bumpy road.

Friendly
Amazing birds fly up together in the beautiful starry sky
Full up with a moon.

Helpfully
Raindrops swiftly side to side
Landing on coloured petals and falling to the ground.

Charlie Heaton (7)
Mount Pleasant Primary School, Brierley Hill

THE STORM

The people run away but they can't escape the storm.
Animals hide in the caves, trembling rapidly.
People cry out, 'The storm is here!' they weep and run into the hut.
It starts to rumble, the rain starts to drip.

But water gives us life.

The water blows, the rain starts to go wild,
The demon and devil come out to play.
The lightning flashes like an arrow darting down to the ground.
The snake rattles and crackles with the demon and devil.
It's wild, it's angry with its tail, it knocks down trees.

But water gives us life.

It died down with a crash and a mash
The devil and demon go away and come back another day.
It's dead and the sun comes out to play
The people come out and say, 'Hey, hey, the storm's gone.'
But water gives us life.

Emma Paynter (10)
Mount Pleasant Primary School, Brierley Hill

BACK IN TIME

In the life of human men,
Travels a traveller from far away
To the world of Tudor town.

Alone in the village
He cannot be heard
Nor can he be seen.

Smoking on the wooden door, he stands,
In frost and snow
As time passed by, he disappeared.

I wonder if the house contained
Anybody dwelling in there alone?
I guess I'll never know.

He wrote a poem
About this day.
You might ask where it is?

It's here right in front of you
You've just finished reading it too.

Lisa Henderson (10)
Mount Pleasant Primary School, Brierley Hill

I Am A Storm, I Am Scary, I Give Life To Everything

I am a storm, I am scary, I give life to everything.
I am a snake tall and long
I am a snake big and strong
When I hiss it's very loud
I make this noisy, hissing sound.

I am a storm, I am scary, I give life to everything.
I am a dragon I can fly
I am a dragon making clouds in the black sky
I am a dragon I keep on getting higher and higher.

I am a storm, I am scary, I give life to everything.
I am a bear, I am a hunter
I am a bear, I am a grunter
I am a bear, I eat everything that I can see
I am a bear, I eat everything but nothing, nothing
Can eat me.

I am a storm, I am scary, I give life to everything.

Ben Pedley (10)
Mount Pleasant Primary School, Brierley Hill

BUT I GIVE LIFE TO MANY

A storm is starting,
I make the sky as black as print,
A bear with claws charges across the sky.

But I give life to many.

I fly through the air,
Splashing and crashing as I go,
Then I turn into a tiger
With my teeth bared.

But I give life to many.

I move as fast as a jet
Thunder is my weapon to blind,
Lightning for attack,
I thrash and crash and destroy.

But I give life to many.

I am as cold as the North Pole
I am tired of destruction
I back off,
I die.

Matthew Mifsud (9)
Mount Pleasant Primary School, Brierley Hill

THE HAUNTED HOUSE

The traveller came all alone,
To the darkest part of the wood.
There stood the haunted house,
Covered in a sheet of darkness.

The traveller smote upon the door,
Not knowing what was going to appear.
A ghost he sees by the door,
Staring at the man.

A cry from the man
Disturbed the forest.
All the creatures came out,
To see what was there.

Away with the man,
Far away,
Everyone knew,
He wouldn't be back another day.

Zoe Nock (10)
Mount Pleasant Primary School, Brierley Hill

THE STORM

The storm is a beast, it strikes at night
Its thunderous blast, fearsome might
It destroys everything in its sight.

The blue waves are foamy and frothy crystal-blue
White as ice
Ice-white, cold
Soft as a pillow.

The storm's a lethal weapon
It fights like a warrior at battle.

The storm crashes and clangs and
Bashes in its battle.

Luke Beresford (10)
Mount Pleasant Primary School, Brierley Hill

FROSTY MORNING

The frost was shining on my
Hands
Like sea pearls.

The playground was as shiny as
The sun.

The Beyblades were spinning like
Ice
Skates twirling.

The bell was ringing, ringing
Ringing in my
Ears like a wedding bell.

Danielle Howard (8)
St Anne's RC Primary School, Sutton Coldfield

FROSTY MORNING

The snow was as white as a whiteboard.
The ice was as slippery as a wet metal pencil case.
The air was as cold as a freezer.
As the playtime bell was ringing,
Ringing, ringing,
To send the children
Back in.

Tom Wright (8)
St Anne's RC Primary School, Sutton Coldfield

FROSTY MORNING

The ice was as slippery as soap.
The frost was glistening like glitter in a tube.
My shadow was as black as a blackout in World War II.
As the playtime bell was ringing, ringing, ringing,
The playtime bell was ringing in the snow that day.

Natalie Whitehouse (9)
St Anne's RC Primary School, Sutton Coldfield

FROSTY MORNING

The Beyblades were glimmering like diamonds
The boys were playing games.
The bell was ringing, ringing, ringing.
So the children were upset.

Lucia Thornton (8)
St Anne's RC Primary School, Sutton Coldfield

FROSTY MORNING

The road was as slippery as soap
The wind was gusty as it blew
My fingers were as stiff as rock
My toes were freezing, freezing, freezing,
My toes were freezing all the way to school.

Grace Saunderson (8)
St Anne's RC Primary School, Sutton Coldfield

FROSTY MORNING

The snow was white as paper.
My fingers were colder than ice.
The frost on my window was like frosted snowflakes.
The sun was beaming, beaming, beaming, all day long.
But it couldn't melt the ice.

Lauren Stevenson (9)
St Anne's RC Primary School, Sutton Coldfield

FROSTY MORNING

The frost was glittering on the car
The snow was turning to ice
My fingers felt like they were dead
As my dad was scraping, scraping, scraping
All the ice off the freezing car.

Adam Rattigan (9)
St Anne's RC Primary School, Sutton Coldfield

FROSTY MORNING

The snow was as white as a swan.
The car was frozen like a statue.
The sun was as hot as the fire.
The frost on my window
Was sparkling, sparkling
Sparkling in the sunlight.
My fingers were about to
Drop off.

Amelia Pedley (8)
St Anne's RC Primary School, Sutton Coldfield

FROSTY MORNING

The light beamed through the curtains like
God's light,
The snow glistened like crystals,
My curtains slowly opened like ghosts were
Opening them,
As the snow was creeping, creeping,
Creeping into my heart and soul.

Emily Minchin (8)
St Anne's RC Primary School, Sutton Coldfield

FROSTY MORNING

The playground as slippery as wet soap.
The ice glistened in the shadows of the sun.
My fingers as cold as ice,
as the play time bell was ringing,
ringing, ringing, on that snowy day.

Chloe Matthews (9)
St Anne's RC Primary School, Sutton Coldfield

FROSTY MORNING

The wind was blowing like
The big bad wolf
The beyblades were gleaming
Like diamonds
The bouncy balls flew up in
The air like snowballs
And the bell came
Ringing
Ringing
Ringing
To send all the children
Back in.

Adam Goldthorp (8)
St Anne's RC Primary School, Sutton Coldfield

FROSTY MORNING

The ice was as cold as a
Fridge.
The snow was white as
Paper.
The frozen water was
Shining
Shining
Shining
The frozen water was
Shining like thousands of
Crystals.

Daniel O'Doherty (9)
St Anne's RC Primary School, Sutton Coldfield

FROSTY MORNING

The ice was as slippery as banana skin
The snow as fluffy as clouds
The children, shouting, shouting
Shouting,
The children were all shouting
Shaking the playground floor.

Rhys Jones (8)
St Anne's RC Primary School, Sutton Coldfield

FROSTY MORNING

The ice was scratching
Like a piece of new chalk,
The snow was as soft
As cotton wool
And my car engine
Was rattling, rattling, rattling,
As my mom scraped off the ice.

Sam Griffith-Allen (9)
St Anne's RC Primary School, Sutton Coldfield

FROSTY MORNING

The snow was as white as the moon
The ice was as slippery as a banana skin
The sun was as yellow as cheese.

The car was not starting, starting, starting
The car was not starting, starting at all.

Cameron Gemmell (8)
St Anne's RC Primary School, Sutton Coldfield

FROSTY MORNING

The spoons were ringing
like the playtime bell
The snow was like an ice ball
The ice made me slither
everywhere like a skateboard.

As I walked out of my
house my teeth were
rattling, rattling,
rattling.
I thought they would fall out.

Blane Cremin-Cullen (9)
St Anne's RC Primary School, Sutton Coldfield

FROSTY MORNING

The ice was strong as metal
The windscreen wipers were
Not moving.
The classroom was like an
Oven.
Mom was
Scraping
Scraping
Scraping
The ice off the car!

James Graydon (8)
St Anne's RC Primary School, Sutton Coldfield

FROSTY MORNING

I woke up as cold as black ice on the long main roads
Outside my frosty window was the deepest,
Bestest, iciest snow of all.
I stood there all frozen
While my alarm clock was ringing, ringing
Ringing

The alarm clock was ringing as loudly as a crow's call.

Hannah Dunne (9)
St Anne's RC Primary School, Sutton Coldfield

FROSTY MORNING

The ice was as hard as a rock.
The sun was a blinding beam of light.
The frost was sparkling in the playground.
As the playtime bell was ringing, ringing, ringing.
As the children marched quickly in.

Tadeusz Forys (8)
St Anne's RC Primary School, Sutton Coldfield

PUPPIES

Scampering around
All over the place
White, brown and black
With a little cute face.
They romp and they chase,
They scamper and play tag.
At night, they cuddle up.
In daytime, tails wag.

Megan Humphrey (8)
St Anne's RC Primary School, Sutton Coldfield

MY DAD

My dad is fat and he hates the name Pat
He's always going on about videos
And he always sleeps with pillows.

My dad is nice sometimes,
Although he hates ice.
My dad does not light candles, but he hates scandals.

Sarina Samra (8)
St Anne's RC Primary School, Sutton Coldfield

FROSTY MORNING

The snow was as white as paper.
The ice was as hard as a rock.
The sun was
Glistening, glistening, glistening.
My toes were as cold as
Antarctica.

Ryan Brough (9)
St Anne's RC Primary School, Sutton Coldfield

FROSTY MORNING

The start of the morning was like
living in an icicle.
The snow was too cold to pick up with
gloves on.
The ice was colder than the North Pole.
It got colder, colder, colder up to the
school gate door.

Seamus Delaney (8)
St Anne's RC Primary School, Sutton Coldfield

IN OUR PLAYGROUND . . .

Children bully, thump and knees bump
They fight in night till midnight
We kick and kill . . .
In our playground!

We play tig
We play cops and robbers
But fight! . . .
In our playground!

School out
Go out away
From bullies . . .
In *our* playground!

Toby Duckworth (8)
St Anne's RC Primary School, Sutton Coldfield

FROSTY MORNING

The icicle was dripping, dripping like
a tear from an eye.

The snow was freezing, freezing like
ice cream.

The teachers were slipping, slipping
on the ice.

The wind was whittling, whittling
like echoes in a cave.

George Bentley (8)
St Anne's RC Primary School, Sutton Coldfield

IN OUR PLAYGROUND . . .

Children are out. Bullies shout.
They whisper
They thump
In our playground!
We run, we jump
We give them a thump
And they bump and jump
In our playground!
The bullies are big
And they look like a pig
In *our* playground!

James Groves (8)
St Anne's RC Primary School, Sutton Coldfield

FROSTY MORNING

The wind was as cold as Antarctica
The garden pond was as slippery as
Banana skins
The neighbour's bird pond was
Glistening,
Glistening,
Glistening
And the birds were wanting a wash but
Couldn't.

Marek Barnes (9)
St Anne's RC Primary School, Sutton Coldfield

WHEN THE STORM ARISES

When the storm arises
People get killed, trees fall down.

When the storm arises,
Telephone wires snap,
Phones, computers and lights go bust.

When the storm arises,
It makes a loud bang and whirls
Things in the air.

When the storm arises,
It lifts cars, houses, bridges, trains and trees
It moves like mad.

When the storm arises,
Inside is safe (a bit)
Outside is a terror.

Jamie Brannigan (8)
St Anne's RC Primary School, Sutton Coldfield

WHEN THE SNOW FALLS

When the snow falls
Birds fly south
When the snow falls
Water turns to ice
When the snow falls
People turn the fire on
When the snow falls
Animals start to hibernate.

Jonathan Hobbs (8)
St Anne's RC Primary School, Sutton Coldfield

MY FAMILY

My mum,
She's not dumb
She likes plums
She's number one
So come on.

My dad,
Now he's bad.

My auntie
When it is bedtime
I cry for tea
She will get it for me
As fast as a bee.

My sister
She's called Abbi
She's always happy
And very snappy.

That's my family
OK, they're mine,
And we're always on time.
Bye! I've got to go, I'm covered
In slime!

Bethany Hague (8)
St Anne's RC Primary School, Sutton Coldfield

COLOURS

The grass is green,
The sky is blue.
Monkeys are clever,
People are too!

The sun is yellow,
Advent is purple.
Nothing is slower,
Than a turtle!

The sky is black,
Pink is nice.
But not as nice,
As sugar and spice!

Emma O'Hanlon (8)
St Anne's RC Primary School, Sutton Coldfield

IN OUR PLAYGROUND

Children play and do what I say.
They run around and sit on the ground.
We run from gangs because they're coming
In our playground!
We scribble on people's homework.
We don't care.
We have no time to stand in the office.
In our playground.
It is fun being naughty and I am the ruler of the gang.
It's fun you know.

Bethany Canavan (8)
St Anne's RC Primary School, Sutton Coldfield

WHAT IS ICE?

The ice is a glimmering scream
Glowing in the moonlight.

A cold lake
Floating in the sky.

It is a winter wolf
Howling in the moonlight.

Jamie Guest (10)
St Martin's CE Primary School, Bilston

WHAT IS SNOW?

A sparkly raindrop only white,
Pouring itself from the sky at night.

Puffs of tiny white balloons falling from Heaven,
And always coming down seven by seven.

A piece of the cloud fallen from the dusky grey sky,
And every child says, 'Oh my!'

Nicole Pearson (10)
St Martin's CE Primary School, Bilston

WHAT IS THE SNOW?

Snow is a white bar of chocolate
Melting on the ground
Snow is a white blanket
Covering the ground
Snow is sugar scattered on the ground.

Mitchell Keown (9)
St Martin's CE Primary School, Bilston

THE CRAZY CLOWN

The crazy clown
Started to jiggle up and down.
He noticed that he lost a skittle
Then he started to cry a little.
The crazy clown started to jump up and down,
He tried to jump so high.
He really wanted to touch the sky.
He was hanging off a cloud,
Then he started to shout out loud.
'Help me, help me, help me please,
Because I have got shivering knees.'
When he came down, he started to cry.
'I don't believe it I,
Have been way up high,
I did touch a cloud.'
Then he started to jig around.

Laura Price (10)
St Martin's CE Primary School, Bilston

A POLAR BEAR

A polar bear who couldn't write,
Sat there crying upon the night.
He sobbed, he sobbed, he sobbed so bad,
How he couldn't write, oh it was sad.
Then he learned, oh it was fun,
He learned his daughter, he learned his son,
He learned his mother, he learned his dad,
And from this day he was not sad.

Laura Pearce (11)
St Martin's CE Primary School, Bilston

MY FOUR SEASONS

I like summer, with the warmth of the sun.
Holidays on the beach can be so much fun.
Lovely big ice creams, to keep you cool.
A sunhat to wear, as I'm no fool.

I like autumn, seeing the leaves turn to gold.
Lying on the ground that the trees used to hold.
The weather is so windy, you could lose your hat.
Hold on tight, or you could get blown flat.

I like winter so chilly and cold.
Building a snowman, so big and so bold.
Watch out for Jack Frost he's ready to bite.
Or you'll end up in bed with a flu to fight.

My favourite season has to be spring,
The birds come back ready to sing.
Everything is changing especially the ground,
Plants are growing, just take a look around.

Lauren Timmins (10)
St Martin's CE Primary School, Bilston

A DAY BENEATH THE SUNSHINE

It shined upon myself
As I watched it light up the sky
I always like to sit in the sunshine
But I don't know why
If I look at it too long it begins
To make me cry.
Sometimes it makes me sweat
But when it's not up the weather is wet.

Sophie Richards (10)
St Martin's CE Primary School, Bilston

WHAT ARE WE?

We are good and bad,
But if we look deep down inside of us
We shall always find more good than bad.
Our touch so sensitive,
Our love so strong,
We are the beat that carries on.

Sian Callaghan (11)
St Martin's CE Primary School, Bilston

AS STRONG AS . . .

As strong as vinegar spilt on your chips.
As strong as a bull stabbing your heart.
As strong as a punch round your cheek.
As strong as salt in your mouth.
As strong as a scorpion stabbing your hand.
As strong as smoke making you cough.
As strong as a kick at your leg.
As strong as a wolf howling in your ear.

Aaron Asprey (8)
St Martin's CE Primary School, Bilston

WHAT IS WIND?

Breath of giant, bending trees.
Motorbike roaring, blowing smoke out.
A big plane roaring past, swirling dust.
Express train whizzing past a wiggly tunnel.
Roaring of a dinosaur howling down the chimney.

Jamie Arrowsmith (10)
St Martin's CE Primary School, Bilston

WHEN THE ELEPHANT WENT TO SCHOOL!

When the elephant went to school
It caused lots of fuss
And hullabaloo.

The staff started shouting,
At that big thing
Their mouths were seriously aching.

The children were frightened
Because the big creature
Had ate all of their maths books.

The nursery were laughing
(But not the teachers)
To see the elephant
Put on a brave show.

Then he went home
And everyone agreed
That it was a very hard day
At school.

When the elephant went to school
It caused lots of fuss
And hullabaloo.

Amy Shepherd (11)
St Martin's CE Primary School, Bilston

SCHOOL

I got up one morning to go to school
But Mum and Dad said I was being a fool
They said I should go out and play
There's no school, today it is Saturday.

Now it is Monday, off to school I go
'What will I learn?' I do not know.
I'll go into class and do my best
And hope it is good enough to pass the test.

The next day teacher lay in wait
As I arrived I was ten minutes late.
She said, 'I think I should mention
For being late you will get detention.'

The next day I arrived on time
The teacher was happy she said that was fine
No detention for me on this day
So it's off home early and time to play.

Cleveland McGrory (8)
St Martin's CE Primary School, Bilston

MY BIRTHDAY

My birthday is in April
It comes once a year, and I have lots of
Nice things.

I have a party with a cake and candles
Balloons and games and fun with my friends.

It always makes me sad when my birthday ends.

My birthday!

Holly Albutt (8)
St Martin's CE Primary School, Bilston

NICKY'S DEVILS

Nicky's in the toilet, the devils will be there,
Nicky said to one devil, 'I will give you a dare.
Watch behind you, there's a bear.
I don't want you to get hurt because I care.'
The teacher's in the classroom,
The devils are so scared.
Nicky's in the playground having a fight,
The devils come along and gave her a big fright.
Nicky is writing sentences,
The devils say to her that light is so bright.

Christopher Bryan & Louie Pullen (9)
St Martin's CE Primary School, Bilston

PANTOMIME

Me and my friends are in pantomime,
It's lots of hard work, but we're having a good time.
Ali Baba is the name of the show,
It was picked by the audience last year you know.
We couldn't find forty, but we have got three thieves,
And the baddies have got some tricks up their sleeves.
My sister is in it, and my mum and dad too,
My sister's a genie, and her costume is blue.
We're the Harem Scarems, me and my friends,
And our singing sends the audience all round the bend.
Everyone laughs and has so much fun,
I am definitely doing another one!

Benjamin Conboy (8)
St Peter's Primary School, Melton Mowbray

MONTHS

January's frost is cold and clear
February is damp and dear
The snowdrops once again are here
March brings the wind and trees blow about
April arrives and the flowers come out
May is fun with two Bank holidays
June is warm with long, sunny days
July brings the end of school
So we can spend August in the pool
September arrives, how summer did fly
October is here, our pumpkins we buy
November brings with it those long, dark nights
December at last, we see those Christmas lights.

James Campbell (8)
St Peter's Primary School, Melton Mowbray

WINTER THOUGHTS

Snow stings just like a bee
Snowballs fly, sledges fall down the hill.
Crack of ice being smashed
The happy laughter of children
Having the time of their lives.
Crunch, as you walk in the snow,
People making snowmen with a happy smile.
Snowflakes glistening in the sunlight,
I'll be sad when it all disappears.

Nicholas Beech (9)
St Peter's Primary School, Melton Mowbray

MY RIDDLE

H   overing above the beautiful ground,
E   veryone has a different sound;
L   oud or silent,
I   mpassive or violent.
C   hopping air as they wander around.
O   n and on, it flies so far,
P   rofessional tricks, hard as a car;
T   wisting and turning,
E   ngines burning.
R   umours about them, can you guess what they are?

Connell Watkins (10)
St Peter's Primary School, Melton Mowbray

MY HARVEST POEM

Packets and tins, fruit and veg
Are things that we all bring,
Flowers and poems, prayers and thoughts
And happy songs we sing.
So celebrate this harvest time
As we all come together,
And give praise and thank God,
That we all have food forever.

Vicky Oliver (9)
St Peter's Primary School, Melton Mowbray

WINTER THOUGHTS

White snow falling on the trees and ground,
Sometimes snowflakes might be found.
On the grass children play,
Running to and fro, to show the way.
Ponds and rivers are covered in ice
For the skaters, very nice.
Temperatures below freezing,
Younger children wheezing.
Dangerous for the cars to drive
Takes them longer to arrive.
In England it hardly ever snows
Still sometimes the child goes
Enjoying the crispy snow.
Buildings get covered, look so white
Usually falls off - it might.
Grass is solid, rock-hard,
Still the wind blows a card.
Maybe cars might have crashed
So the helicopters come to see if they're
Smashed.

George Moore (9)
St Peter's Primary School, Melton Mowbray

GOLD

Gold is . . .
The sun shining through
A fish glittering in the water
A crown on a king's head
The golden goal that wins the cup
A door waiting to be opened
A light welcoming you home.

Charlie Lang (9)
Windmill House School, Oakham

WINTER

The soft feel of the crunchy snow
The feel of the wind when it's starting to blow.
The feel of gloves all warm and soft,
Getting the decorations from up in the loft.
The smell of mince pies, sweet and sour
The look of the first winter flower.
The snowdrops shooting out of the ground
The howl of the wind, a threatening sound.
The naked trees, leaves long gone,
Birds migrating to the hot sun.
Robins stay at home.
The wet dog trying to get at his bone.
He gets called inside, all wet and soggy.
The next morning it's very foggy.
All the snow melts away,
But it'll be back another day.

Bianca Gillam (8)
Windmill House School, Oakham

FIRST SNOW OF WINTER

The first snow of winter came early one night.
The weatherman had said, and of course he was right.
A frosty morning, a blizzard started,
By twelve o'clock the storm had departed.
I made a snowman on the ground,
Later on, he had spread around.
Lots of fun with our snowball fight,
Stay for a while, world of white.

William Crossley (10)
Windmill House School, Oakham

MY ROOM IS...

My room is small but very wide.
Wardrobe on the left and bed by the side.
My room is cosy,
My bed is snug
There's only one problem,
I'm scared at midnight.
My room is yellow and red and green.
My room is orange, purple and pink.
My room is quiet, quiet as a spy,
My room is full of bugs, bees and butterflies.
My carpet is green, my floor is brown,
At midnight there are threatening sounds.
All my shelves lined up in a row,
Toy rockets and planes ready to go.
My room is bright and my room is dark,
Dark only at night.

George Norton (8)
Windmill House School, Oakham

SNOW

Snow has fallen through the night,
Covering the world with a blanket of white.
Hills look like scoops of vanilla ice cream.
Frozen lakes glisten and gleam.
Creatures leave footprints in the snow,
The biting wind begins to blow.
Wrap up warm, go out to play,
Hope the snow won't go away.

Emily Morgan (11)
Windmill House School, Oakham

MY LOST CAT

When my mummy came into the class
She was crying lots and lots
I hadn't a clue what was wrong.

Suddenly she told me,
'Your cat has run away,
We lost him at the vet's.'

We rushed to Market Harborough
And went to look for him.

We could not find my cat
Each day I hope that he'll come home
So every day he's not alone.

Christopher Lane (8)
Windmill House School, Oakham

MAGPIE

A thief by night, a spy by day,
Waiting for people to go away.
A jewel thief may be near you.
Gold and silver, jewels too.
In his black and white suit,
He lurks in the night not making a sound.
Watching and waiting for whatever's around.
Things are missing, no trace can be found,
The silent thief - he's not around!

Freddie Oliver (10)
Windmill House School, Oakham

STORM

He's escaped!
That horrible Mr Storm.

The children start to cry,
He's spoiling their fun
By crying on their heads.

The winter's fresh air
Has been spoilt by his anger.
Leaves start to fall,
Windows start to shatter.

Soon his anger gets worse and worse.
He starts to throw shining spears at the poor trees.
And then there's a crash of tiles,
What a clatter!

But now the sun tries to come out,
To face this opponent.
They start to fight and Storm is defeated.
He slouches away
Back to his cloudy home.

James Henley (9)
Windmill House School, Oakham

GOLD

Gold is . . .
A trophy after a game
A leaf on the ground
A feather off a bird
A smile to a mother
A kiss to a wife
A tear to a child.

Joseph Harrap (9)
Windmill House School, Oakham

My School

It's happy,
It's joyful,
It's full of life.
It's called Windmill House,
And it's really nice.
It's kind of my home, in a way
I go there to work, every weekday.
Our head teacher is really nice,
My form is Form 4,
And it's full of life.
It's bustling with children,
Some short and some tall,
There's paintings and pictures
Hung up on the wall.
Posters and borders surround all our work.
The chalk board and chalks,
Pots full of paint.
If I have to say,
I think my school's
                    Great!

Holly Singlehurst (9)
Windmill House School, Oakham

Gold

Gold is . . .
A ring glistening in the light
The sun shining in the sky
A knight's shield guarding him from darkness
A watch given to me by my dad
The feeling when I'm happy or excited
Pride when I've done something I haven't done before.

Matthew Ramsden (9)
Windmill House School, Oakham

SNOW

I can walk across your garden
Not waking anything in sight.
Fluttering everywhere,
Covering everything.
You wake up in the morning
And see that I have been there
Because my blanket has been left behind.
Then the sun comes out
And he makes a mess of my lovely white world.
So I go away, feeling sad
As he has destroyed my day.

Tristan Roper-Caldbeck (9)
Windmill House School, Oakham

ICE

She touches a river with her long, spiky
fingers to turn it into ice.
She pulls people down on the slippery pavement.
She makes things glisten like stars.
The ground looks like glass.
She chokes plants with her freezing, icy breath.
She leaves icicles hanging from the gutters above.
Now she's off to another place.
The sun comes out and melts it all.
I think she'll be back again . . .
Some day.

Ellie McRoberts (9)
Windmill House School, Oakham

SNOW

When I woke up this morning
She'd covered everything in sight.
She'd crept over the garden, the trees,
the house and the fence.
She'd turned the flowers into lumps of
cotton wool,
She'd turned the roads from black to white,
The rushes by the pond to lollipops.
Even the house turned into a gigantic brick.
Suddenly the sun began to rise
So she started to melt away and away,
But I know she'll come back next year.

Sophie Harris (9)
Windmill House School, Oakham

ICE

He touched the river and it froze in seconds.
He blocked the outside tap with his icy fingers.
He blew on the windows so that they froze.
He cast a spell under people's feet.
He sneezed, then black ice came everywhere.
Any gap he saw, he filled.
He laughed at all the mischief he has done.
But then the sun came and melted it all away.
Ice was very angry, but he'll be back again tomorrow night.

Alex Cooke (10)
Windmill House School, Oakham

MONSTER MISCHIEF

I crept across the landing,
Opened up the door,
Closed the door behind me,
And tiptoed across the floor.

I lent against the boiler,
And started to close my eyes,
Then the door started opening,
As silent as a spy.

A shadow shimmered over to the old school desk,
And switched on the light.
When I realised who it was,
My jaw dropped to the floor.

I shouted out as loud as I could,
'Oh Mummy there you are,'
She told me off so deadly,
Took me to my room.

Then she told me with a smile on her face,
'Didn't I ever tell you about the monster in the loft?

He eats people like you!'

Georgia Carr (8)
Windmill House School, Oakham

SNOWY DAYS

Snow is like a dove perched on a tree.
Snowflakes are a smashed window on a car.
Snowfall is a sieve with icing sugar in it.
Snow on a tree is like a man in an evening suit.
Snow is great fun for everyone.

Georgina Cook (11)
Windmill House School, Oakham

MY ROOM

Lots of clothes on the floor,
The yellow paint on the wall,
My desk crammed with stuff.

I love my room,
It's the best,
I love the pictures on the wall.

O the wonder of my room,
It has only just begun,
My little night light's little glow.

Both my medals on a peg,
My little bits on a shelf,
My light's as bright as the morning sun.

All my toys in a basket,
Mummy calling, 'It's time for tea.'
My chest of drawers, as old as me.

The view of the garden from my room,
The little flowers in a vase,
The drawings I drew on the window.

My big doll's house in the corner,
All my stuff is beautiful,
My room is peaceful, O so peaceful.

Amelia Steele (8)
Windmill House School, Oakham